SU̲ ̲ ̲ ̲ ̲ NG

American Indian Literature
and
Critical Studies Series

Gerald Vizenor, General Editor

Other Books by Gerald Vizenor

The People Named the Chippewa: Narrative Histories

Wordarrows: Indians and Whites in the New Fur Trade

Crossbloods: Bone Courts, Bingo, and Other Reports

Interior Landscapes: Autobiographical Myths and Metaphors

Dead Voices: Natural Agonies in the New World

The Heirs of Columbus

Landfill Meditation: Crossblood Stories

Griever: An American Monkey King in China

Bearheart: The Heirship Chronicles

Summer in the Spring
*Anishinaabe Lyric Poems
and Stories
New Edition*

Edited and Interpreted by
Gerald Vizenor

University of Oklahoma Press
Norman and London

Riverside Community College
Library
4800 Magnolia Avenue
AUG   '95   Riverside, California 92506

PM854.Z95 S95 1993
Summer in the spring :
Anishinaabe lyric poems and
stories

tion Data

ems and
Vizenor —

New ed.

    p.   cm. — (American Indian literature and
critical studies series ; v. 6)
   Includes bibliographical references.
   ISBN 0-8061-2518-7
   1. Ojibwa poetry — Translations into English.
2. Ojibwa Indians — Legends.   3. Ojibwa Indians —
Religion and mythology. I. Vizenor, Gerald Robert,
1934— . II. Series.
PM854.Z95S95   1993
897'.3 — dc20   92-32561
                                 CIP

The paper in this book meets the guidelines for
permanence and durability of the Committee on
Production Guidelines for Book Longevity of the
Council on Library Resources, Inc.

*Summer in the Spring: Anishinaabe Lyric Poems and
Stories, New Edition*, is Volume 6 in the American
Indian Literature and Critical Studies Series.

Published by the University of Oklahoma Press,
Norman, Publishing Division of the University.
Copyright © 1965, 1970, 1981, 1993 by Gerald Vizenor.
All rights reserved. Manufactured in the U.S.A. First
printing of the University of Oklahoma Press edition,
1993.

1 2 3 4 5 6 7 8 9 10

IN MEMORY OF MY FATHER

Clement William Vizenor

if you wish to know me
you must seek me in the clouds

i am a bird
who rises from the earth and flies
far up into the skies
out of human sight

though not visible to the eye
my voice is heard from afar
and resounds over the earth

KEESHKUMUN
Anishinaabe Orator

Contents

SUMMER IN THE SPRING

Introduction

"The clear sky loves to hear me sing" is a heartened invitation to the tribal dream songs translated as lyric poems in this book. The dreamers listen to the turnout of the seasons, and the everlasting sky hears their voices on the wind.

The dream songs were the signatures of personal and communal woodland identities. "With a large bird above me, I am walking in the sky" is one avian vision that was heard with other distinctive woodland songs in *anishinaabemowin*, the oral language of the *anishinaabe*.

There were worried hearts that recovered memories, and trickster stories that endured the manifest manners of a consumer civilization. The dreams heard in these songs and lyric poems are primal unions with tribal contradictions, unstudied creations, chance, and natural reasons. The loneliness of civilization, the tragic burdens of silence, and buried seasons came with romantic revisions and the measured ruins of nativism.

Written languages and translations were contradictions in most tribal communities, chances to overcome tragic reason and the loss of

tribal memories. The visions of birds and words
once heard were roused in the imagination and
remembrance of readers, a new tribal
hermeneutics. The translations and
interpretations in this collection are the
remembered shadows of the heard visions and
stories of tribal survivance, the memories that
walk with birds in the sky and sing across the
water. These memories are the primal union of
visions, humor, and stories.

The translation from the heard to the written
is a transvaluation of the heard to the seen, the
listener once and the reader evermore. Those
who heard stories were hounded to the sense of
the present; the bent of communal remembrance
was never the same. Tribal stories in translation,
however, are tributes to that sense of the present
that is abandoned to the weakness of historical
time. The visions, scenes, and seasons once heard
in tribal stories were broken on ideologies, and
overturned in revisions that counted too much
on the assurance of cultural permanence.

"The sky resounds when I come making a
sound," is a tribal bounce and vision that cannot
be denied in translation; the pompous pronoun is
a trickster signature, an ironic oral mediation on
creation and tribal identities.

The sacred *miigis*, the cowrie of creation in the
stories of the woodland tribes, arose from the
eastern sea and moved the seasons over the

inland waters. The *anishinaabe* pursued the
miigis cowrie and original tribal totems with
giizis, the sun, to a place named *bawitig*, the
long rapids in the river.

The *anishinaabe* (the plural is *anishinaabeg*),
the original *miigis* people of the woodland, heard
natural wisdom in their stories, and the colors of
the seasons were given to the tribes by the sun
on the back of the sacred cowrie. The reflection
warmed the tribes on their long migration from
the eastern sea. More than five hundred years ago
the *miigis* appeared in the sun for the last time at
mooningwanekaning, or *mooningwane*, the place
of the yellow-shafted flicker, in *anishinaabe
gichigami*, Lake Superior, the great sea of the
original five tribal families of the *anishinaabe*.

The *anishinaabe* learned to hear the seasons
by natural reason, and tribal dreamers heard the
stories of creation in *bangishimog noodin*, the
west wind, their relations to the animals, birds,
stones, the heat of visions, and the everlasting
circles of the sun and moon and human heart.
The first tribal families trailed the shores of
gichigami to the hardwoods and marshes
where they touched the maple trees for
ziizibaakwadaaboo in the spring, speared fish on
the rivers, and then gathered *manoomin*, wild
rice, in the late autumn. Before winter and the
cold snow the tribes returned to their
communities at *mooningwanekaning* on

Madeline Island in Lake Superior. The *anishinaabe* told trickster stories of the summer heart as the snow covered the red pine and the rivers froze.

The old world was a rumor of demonic seasons, seldom a source of tribal inspiration, and the vicious outcome of colonial invasions, discoveries, diseases, and the territorial boundaries levied on the woodland have never been absolved in the duplicities of treaties and histories.

In the seventeenth century the voyageurs and the first missionaries established a fur trading post at *mooningwanekaning* on Madeline Island. The christian community was situated near the sacred burial sites of the *anishinaabe.* While showing the discoverers how to endure the cold winters, more than half of the tribal families on the island died in a smallpox epidemic, the first recorded pestilence brought by the *gichi mookomaanag*, or *chimookomaan*, the white people and their missionaries.

The latinization of the woodland tribes was measured by compulsive and passionate missionaries who shouted the epistles and secured their cold manners over the natural wisdom of dreamers and healers; the charitable missions attainted the tribes to a nether generation of savagism.

Lethal pathogens and recurrent epidemics

weakened the dreamers and tribal healers. Vulnerable woodland families were bound to hear the hymns of monotheism. The nervy voyageurs traded their nationalism and ironic praise of salvation for the hides of animals. The fur traders learned the languages and stories of the woodland and enmeshed tribal families in the predatory economics of peltry.

The elaborate political and economic interests of the fur trade, spurred by the distant bourgeois demand for felt hats, summoned tribal hunters and trappers to new trading posts, a precursor of consumer sacrifices to a chemical civilization, with beaver peltry as barter for firearms, diluted intoxicants, and trivial baubles.

The *anishinaabe* used their new firearms to defeat other woodland tribes. The Dakota, for instance, were driven south and westward, out of the richest wild rice areas.

> *moving forward and back*
> *from the woodland to the prairie*
> *dakota women*
> *weeping*
> *as they gather*
> *their wounded men*
> *the sound of their weeping*
> *comes back to us*

The woodland fur trade interposed economic anomalies between the intuitive rhythms of woodland tribal communities and the spiritual

equipoise of the traditional *anishinaabe*.
Millions of tribal families died in the epidemics,
and as the tribes relumed their human unities
and healed the communities, thousands of
immigrants procured the land with new laws and
liens of a constitutional democracy. The
anishinaabe were enslaved once more by the
furies of the colonists and the terminal creeds of
landholders.

> *honoring your brave men*
> *like them*
> *believing in myself*

Christian patriotism and the harsh cadence of
national destinies crushed the wild seasons and
overcame the earth and tribal cultures. The
anishinaabe families of the *maang*, loon, the
people of the *makwa*, bear, and those who were
related to the *amik*, beaver, were denied the
power of their visions and separated from their
woodland languages. At the same time the
missionaries stole the natural wisdom of the
tribes, and the emissaries of righteous action
unfurled the banners of religious and political
freedom.

> *brave warriors*
> *where have you gone*
> *ho kwi ho ho*

The *anishinaabe* heard their histories as stories, a source of natural reason and traditional esteem. Written histories came much later and misconstrued tribal encounters with the *gichi mookomaanag*. The past was heard in the present; the dream songs and stories carried the natural sounds of visual memories. Dreams, visions, and the touch of heard stories bound the everlasting identities of the woodland tribes to chance and the seasons of animals and stones. Stories are the eternal creations of liberation.

Keeshkemun told the *zhaaganaashag*, the Englishmen, "If you wish to know me you must seek me in the clouds." The military officers had asked the elder to explain his position in the woodland territorial wars. The *anishinaabe* orator responded to the *zhaaganaashag* with a personal dream song that has become one of the common stories of tribal liberation. "I am a bird who rises from the earth and flies far up into the skies out of human sight, though not visible to the eye, my voice is heard from afar and resounds over the earth."

The *anishinaabe* heard stories in their dream songs. Tribal visions were natural sources of intuition and identities, and some tribal visions were spiritual transmigrations that inspired the lost and lonesome souls of the woodland to be healed.

the first to come
epithet among the birds
bringing the rain
crow is my name

The *anishinaabe* heard visions in the stories of animals, birds, wind, trees, insects, the sound of seasons, and in the thunder of ice on the lakes. The stories of nature were heard in names. Place names and personal nicknames were communal stories. The *anishinaabe* were never alone in their names, visions, and stories.

the wind
only
fearing him

across the earth
everywhere
making my voice heard

The *anishinaabe* word for the oral language is *anishinaabemowin*. The performance of the trickster stories is natural wisdom; that creative sense of motion is in the present. The hermeneutics of trickster stories are the motion of the seasons, the language games, avian visions, crows in the winter birch, and the ironic amusement of overstated personal pronouns.

my feathers
sailing
on the breeze

the clear sky
loves to hear me sing

overhanging clouds
echoing my words
with a pleasing sound

The words in *anishinaabemowin* are
euphonious: *anishinaabe nagamon*, songs of the
people; *nibi*, water; *makwa*, bear; *bibigwan*,
flute; *manoomin*, wild rice; *gimiwan*, it is
raining; *ziibiwan*, rivers; *memengwaag*,
butterflies; *giiweniibin*, late summer;
giiwebiboon, late winter; *ishkode*, fire;
bapakine, grasshopper; *waawaatesi*, firefly;
miigwani wiiwakwaan, feather headdress;
manidoo, a spirit.

The *anishinaabe* drew pictures of their dream
songs, visions, stories, and ideas on birchbark.
The song pictures of the *midewiwin*, the religion
of tribal healers, were incised on the soft inner
bark of the birch. These scrolls of dream song
pictures, or pictomyths, are sacred and heard
only by members of the *midewiwin*, who believe
that visions, songs, and the use of herbal

medicines heal and sustain the human spirit.

> *I am like the spirit*
> *waiting*
> *in my lodge*
> *making me very old*

The *anishinaabe* were driven to silence and the fear of space in their dream songs and stories; the names and ceremonies connected humans and animals to the earth and to the communal memories of the tribe; time was heard in the present and not the cause of terminal incertitudes. The personal visions that were unbroken in the extremes of nature would seldom be heard in mere isolation, and meditation would never lead to the common fears of separation, manifest manners, and the loneliness of civilization; chance, the touch of trickster stories, and the inspiration of contradictions, were natural, perilous, and serious sources of communal identities. Tribal relations were created in visions, and those who endured the natural menace of the seasons and the chance of ecstasies could become healers and shamans.

> *brave warriors*
> *where have you gone*
> *ho kwi ho ho*

The *anishinaabe* stories and dream songs are heard as the voices of individual freedom; in published translations the songs are lyric poems and the stories are a new tribal hermeneutics and literature.

The stories in this book about the *midewiwin* and the birth and death of *naanabozho,* that figuration of a compassionate tribal trickster, have been heard and remembered by tribal people in many generations; the published versions of these stories are various, and a sense of contradiction is endowed in comparative postcolonial literature.

Most of the stories about the tribal trickster are not sacred, wicked, or wise; rather, the trickster is eternal motion and transformation in the stories. The trickster is boasted on cue and comes to naught; no critical closures, representations, or essential cultural conditions could hold the stories. There are stories named *aadizookaanag,* or traditional stories, but these are not heard as trickster stories. There are trickster creation stories, but these stories are about the comic and ironic nature of humans, animals, and birds in the world.

The *anishinaabe* heard the creation and observance of dream songs and stories in their essential seasons. The trickster stories, in particular, were told as comic mediation and liberation, a trickster hermeneutics, the inimitable language games heard on those cold winter nights when the trickster *naanabozho* was not about to listen in the transformational face of an animal or flower. The selection, edited translations, and interpretations in this book are celebrations of oral literature. At the same time, this publication should be a reminder that there are as many versions of tribal dream songs and stories as there are listeners and readers.

The stories in this book were first translated and printed more than a century ago in *The Progress*, a weekly newspaper that was published on the White Earth Reservation in Minnesota.

The first issue of *The Progress* was published and distributed on March 25, 1886, eighteen years after hundreds of tribal families were removed by treaty from other areas of the woodland to the new federal exclave named the White Earth Reservation. The editor and publisher announced that the "novelty of a newspaper published upon this reservation may cause many to be wary in their support, and this from a fear that it may be revolutionary in character. . . . We shall aim to advocate constantly and withhold reserve, what in our view, and in the view of the leading minds upon this reservation, is the best for the interests of its residents. And not only for their interests, but those of the tribe wherever they now are residing."

Indian agents were not pleased to honor the language of rights or the most common demonstration of the First Amendment to the Constitution of the United States. The federal agents confiscated *The Progress* and ordered the removal of two tribal members, the editor, Theodore Hudon Beaulieu, and the publisher, Augustus Hudon Beaulieu, from the White Earth Reservation. The second issue of *The Progress* was distributed about six months later, once a federal district court ruled that the newspaper should be published on a federal reservation without interference.

The stories edited and interpreted in this book were first published in an eleven-part series in *The Progress* between December 1887 and May 1888. The newspaper was circulated to tribal members on the reservation. A decade later *The Progress* became *The Tomahawk* and circulation grew to several thousand subscribers on reservations and in cities.

Theodore Hudon Beaulieu wrote in the original introduction to the series published in *The Progress* that two members of the

midewiwin, Day Dodge and Saycosegay, told
stories of the religious life of the tribe in
anishinaabemowin, the oral language of the
anishinaabe. The stories were then translated by
the editor and published under his name. These
are oral versions of the trickster stories; the
author does not indicate when he first heard the
stories. The editor and publisher of *The Progress*
were both crossblood members of the tribe and
lived on the White Earth Reservation.

Day Dodge was said to be over ninety years old
when his stories about the *midewiwin* were
published in *The Progress.* In other words, he was
born before the turn of the nineteenth century,
before treaties and the removal of the tribes to
federal exclaves and reservations.

The *anishinaabemowin* words have been
italicized for critical attention to the written
transcription of an oral tribal language. The
orthographic transcription of words in
anishinaabemowin conforms to the precise
entries in *Ojibwewi-Ikidowinan: An Ojibwe
Word Resource Book* (Saint Paul: Minnesota
Archaeological Society, 1979), edited by John
Nichols and Earl Nyholm at Bemidji State
University in Minnesota.

Nichols wrote: "Ojibwe and the other
languages grouped together in the Algonquian

language family resemble each other so closely
in sound patterns, grammar, and vocabulary that
at one time they must have been a single
language: as the speakers of this ancient
language, no longer spoken, became separated
from one another, the way they spoke changed in
different ways until we have the distinct
language spoken today. . . . At the time of the
European invasion of North America, the
languages of the Algonquian language family
were spoken by Indians along the Atlantic coast
from what is now North Carolina to
Newfoundland, inland across Canada to the
Great Plains, and in the region of the Great
Lakes, perhaps ranging as far south as Alabama
and Georgia. . . . Long contact with English and
French, numerically more numerous and
officially dominant, has taken its toll of many of
these languages. The condition of Ojibwe varies
widely. In much of Northwestern and Northern
Ontario and in Manitoba it is spoken by people
of all ages and the actual number of speakers is
increasing as the population grows. In many
Ojibwe communities in the United States and
other parts of Canada it is spoken only by those
middle-aged and older."

The editor and interpreter of the dream songs
and stories in this book has heard songs and

stories in *anishinaabemowin*, but he is not a
primary speaker of a tribal language; he studied
the dictionaries, orthographies, and the various
oral transcriptions. Selected tribal words from
the oral language have been inset to enhance the
translations of the stories.

The interpretation of the stories and
transcriptions of the dream songs entailed the
use of other word lists, language lessons, and
dictionaries. For instance, *A Dictionary of the
Otchipwe Language*, by Frederick Baraga, first
published more than a century ago, and
Chippewa Exercises, by Chrysostom Verwyst,
were significant sources of information on earlier
versions of the language. The Baraga dictionary
contains some words in *anishinaabemowin* that
are no longer spoken, and other words that have
changed in sound and usage in the past century.
Entries in the Baraga dictionary may best reflect
the oral language at the time the dream songs
and stories were heard in tribal communities,
and the time the stories were first transcribed
and translated by Theodore Hudon Beaulieu for
publication in *The Progress.*

The lyric poems in this book were first
published in a limited hardbound edition as
*Summer in the Spring: Lyric Poems of the
Ojibway.* The second, revised, paperbound

edition was published as *Anishinabe Nagamon* by the Nodin Press. The stories, first printed in *The Progress* in the late nineteenth century, also were edited and published in *Anishinabe Adisokan*. A third edition of the poems and a second revised edition of the stories, edited and reexpressed, were combined and published as *Summer in the Spring: Ojibwe Lyric Poems and Tribal Stories* in 1981 by the Nodin Press. This edition has a new introduction and glossary.

The title, *Summer in the Spring*, is a line borrowed from a dream song that was first recorded, transcribed, and translated in *Chippewa Music*, by Frances Densmore (Washington, D. C.: Government Printing Office, 1910). The interpretations of the other dream songs in this book are based on her original records, transcriptions, and translations. Densmore was one of the most sensitive musicologists and ethnologists who recorded the music and songs of the *anishinaabe* and other tribes.

> *as my eyes*
> *look across the prairie*
> *I feel the summer*
> *in the spring*

The use of italicization and lower case for *anishinaabemowin* words is intended to emphasize the values of the oral language rather than a total imposition of the philosophies of grammar and translation. The natural name *anishinaabe* is heard in *anishinaabemowin*, the oral language of the tribe. The Anishinaabe were nominated the Ojibway, the Ojibwe, the Chippewa, Chippeway, and other names in written translations and historical documents.

The illustrations in this book are enlarged photographic reproductions of the original tribal pictomyths that were first published by the Bureau of American Ethnology in two books: *Chippewa Music*, by Frances Densmore, and *The Mide'wiwin or 'Grand Medicine Society' of the Ojibway*, by W. J. Hoffman (Seventh Annual Report [1891], pp. 143–300).

The *anishinaabe* pictomyth on the title page is the story of the sun and the *miigis* in dream songs, the story that heard the *midewiwin* secrets of the heart. The other pictomyths are explained in the Interpretive Notes.

Anishinaabeg
Lyric Poems

as my eyes

look across the prairie

i feel the summer

in the spring

maple sugar

only

satisfies me

in the spring

the first to come

epithet among the birds

bringing the rain

crow is my name

my music

reaching to the sky

great mounds of clouds

over there

where i am looking

the clear sky

resounds

when i come

making a sound

the clear sky

loves to hear me sing

all around

the sky

with my sound

i come to you

overhanging clouds

echoing my words

with a pleasing sound

across the earth

everywhere

making my voice heard

sound of thunder

sometimes

i pity myself

while the wind

carries me

across the sky

those large birds

thunderbirds

surprising me

The tipi lodge in this pictomyth shows the home of the midewiwin spirit. The wavy lines represent the power of music reaching the heart.

going to the south

i will bring

the south wind

in the sky

over there

they have taken pity on me

the turtle

sitting

beside him

two foxes

facing each other

sitting

between them

with a large bird

above me

i am walking

in the sky

i entrust

myself

to one wind

when my midewiwin drum

sounds for me

the sky

clears

the sky is blue

he hi hi hi

when my midewiwin drum

sounds for me

the waters are smooth

ho ho ho ho

what is this i promise you

he hi hi hi

the sky

will be bright and clear

for you

this is what i promise you

ho ho ho ho

i will prove

alone

the power of my spirit

i return

to the lodge of the big bear

it is time

for you to return

i am going

on a long journey

all around the sky

flying

the loons

are singing

i am like the spirit

waiting

in my lodge

making me very old

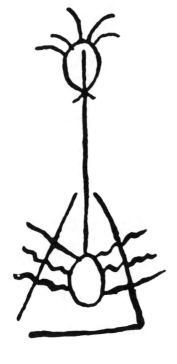

moving forward and back

from the woodland to the prairie

dakota women

weeping

as they gather

their wounded men

the sound of their weeping

comes back to us

thoughts of revenge

soaring

across the sky

when we are dancing

around a dakota scalp

brave old woman

defending her children

she endured

fighting for us all

sound of feet

passing on the prairie

those men

they are playing a game

as they return

whenever i am alone

gookookoo oo

sitting in the wigwam

gookookoo oo

i am very much afraid

of the owl

gookookoo oo

The anishinaabe hunter in this pictomyth is hiding in a blind covered with branches and leaves. A rabbit is placed near the blind as bait in the eyes of the eagle. Swooping down he is caught by the legs. The anishinaabe hunter plucks a few feathers and the eagle is free again.

my feathers

sailing

on the breeze

honoring your brave men

like them

believing in myself

brave warriors

where have you gone

ho kwi ho ho

burial song

neniwa

let us stand

to see my body

as i would like to be seen

hunting

like a little star

i shine

the animals

are held

staring at my light

if i were a son-in-law

i would take on my journey

june berries to eat

let them despise us

we have salt

and live beyond the woods

i am thinking

. . . nia

i am thinking

. . . nia

i have found my lover

. . . nia

i think it is so

the sound of a loon

i thought

it was my lover

paddling

watching my lover

paddling

her canoe

across the lake

i am as beautiful

as the roses

i am going away

today

it is true

i am going away

very soon

i will return

do not weep

it is true

we will be very happy

to meet again

when i return

do not weep

The varying lines on the body of the figure in this
pictomyth show the feelings of a man for the old
woman who sings this song.

my lover

is leaving

for a distant land

soon

he will return

he has departed

to bawitig

the long rapids in the river

gone before me

i will never see

my lover again

i have been waiting

a long time around the drum

for my lover

to come over

where i am sitting

if you go with me

when i leave

i will give you

what you will wear

i am asking

for his oldest daughter

my son is giving

my big brass kettle

naanabozho song

dance and sing

across the water

if you open your eyes

they will turn red

Anishinaabeg
Stories and Tales

The Anishinaabeg

You have asked me to tell you the customs of our ancestors and the origin of the *anishinaabeg*. My grandchild, it is your wish and I shall tell you our beliefs.

The first appearance of our people, the *anishinaabeg*, occurred in this way:

When the great spirit, or *gichimanidoo* made up his mind to create man, he took a handful of earth and rubbed it together in his palms and a man was formed. The *manidoo* below the earth, who was a very imposing *manidoo*, with heavy locks of white hair, said to *gichimanidoo* in counsel: *What are you going to do with only one anishinaabe?* In answer to this question *gichimanidoo* took another handful of earth and rubbed it in his palms and a woman was formed. Then he said, *this person shall be the fruit of the earth, and the seed from which shall come the anishinaabeg people. This my grandchild is how the anishinaabeg originated and became so numerous.*

Naming Children

I shall now tell you our customs regarding the naming of children, and the customs by which their lives are guided. It is believed that every child, while he is in his mother's womb, wonders *what disposition his parents are going to make of him.* When a child is about to be born, his parents begin accumulating provisions and clothing. After his birth his parents hold a feast.

A spokesman is selected by the father who is supposed to act for the child. A meeting of some of the principal men of the tribe is held and it is decided who shall be the *niiawee* — the person to whom the life of the child will be dedicated. It does not always follow that the child will be named after the *niiawee* but he must in the course of time give the child some name.

When the selection of a *niiawee* has been made, the spokeman who has been selected to preside over the meeting, invokes the *gichimanidoo* to guard the future of the *anishinaabe* child and give him a long life.

A pipe with a long decorated stem is lighted, and offered as a sacrifice to the *gichimanidoo* in this way: the stem is first pointed in the direction of the *waaban*, east, the *zhaawans*,

south, the *bangishimog*, west, the *giiwᵉdin*,
north and then downwards towards the earth.
After this ceremony is concluded, the person
who has been selected to name the child is
called in and informed of the duty imposed upon
him.

A *nickname* is generally given by the parents
or some other relative of the child. The *real
name* of the *anishinaabe* child is given only by
his *niiawee*, which is usually done when the
child has become sick for the first time.

My grandchild, it was the custom of our
ancestors to be guided throughout their lives by
their dreams . . . the most important dreams
guided our ancestors. During his life, an
anishinaabe dreams about many animals and
birds and some one of these impress him deeply.
The person who is selected to name a child, tells
the child of some dream about a certain animal
and says, *niiawee will be named after it, and I
will go after the animal which I have told you
about.*

His main object then is to procure the animal
he may have dreamed of, which the
gichimanidoo usually allowed him to secure.
The animal was cooked and served out at a grand
feast for friends and relatives. The *niiawee* then
commences a chant, which has been composed
by him for the occasion, and of words which he
has dreamed of at sometime during his life.

The animal which has been cooked is a peace offering to the *gichimanidoo* by the person who named the child, because he dreamed of this and knew how to conciliate the *gichimanidoo* who permitted the *anishinaabe* child to be born and allowed him to live. The *gichimanidoo* very seldom takes the child away because he pities the *anishinaabe* who have confidence in him. This my grandchild, was the way our *anishinaabe* ancestors named their children.

Anishinaabeg Women

Bakan ishkodawe, which means for a woman, making a fire elsewhere, was a custom followed by *anishinaabeg* women, and was established among them by *naanabozho*, the compassionate tribal trickster, of whom I will have much to say later. It will take a long time to tell about him as all our traditions refer to him. When the earth was covered with water he was the being who formed a new earth. But I am going to speak now of the custom regarding women.

My grandchild, you see by the locks of my hair which have been whitened by the snows of many winters that I am a very aged man, and many, many moons ago the customs which I intend to speak about, were followed by *anishinaabeg* women. Since the old men of our tribe have all dropped away and disappeared from the earth, you never hear that a young girl who has just reached puberty is removed or sent away from a village during the time when nature is changing her from childhood to womanhood. Neither do you ever hear of *bakan ishkodawe* for a woman now. But in those past days our women had strong restrictions placed over them.

When a young girl first became aware of the change nature was about to make with her, she immediately left the village to which she belonged and built at some distance away from it a small lodge of a sufficient size to allow her to lie down comfortably, but not high enough to stand in it. She remained in the *bakan ishkodawe* so long as she could fast, which was from five to ten days. She would not go any distance from her lodge, for if a man crossed her tracks while she was undergoing her transition, he immediately fell to the ground paralyzed and it became necessary for the *mashkikiiwinini* to be called in to cure him.

My grandchild, you cannot properly understand without an illustration, how strong the *manidoog*, spirits, are during this period.

When I was a young man I had many warts on my hands . . . I was almost covered by them. An old woman of my tribe advised me to go to a girl who had built a *bakan ishkodawe* at some distance from our *oodena*, town, and who was undergoing the *giigwishimowin*, fast, or fasting, period, and have her cure me. I disliked the warts very much, and being ashamed of my ugly looking hands, I reluctantly concluded to follow her advice. I was warned about crossing her tracks, and to approach the lodge from the side very carefully, and if I reached it safely to pass my hands in the front and say, *I have come to you to cure my hands.*

I approached the lodge, passed my hands in,

and repeated the words as directed. She wet her fingers with her saliva and touched all the warts on my hands, and when she had completed this, I retraced my steps and returned to the village. In five days all the warts on my hand had disappeared.

While a girl is passing this period she eats nothing of her own volition and not until her mother offers her something, which must be a piece of fresh meat cooked almost to a crisp over living coals of *ishkode*. She will not accept this if she can forego the temptation, for the longer the *giigwishimowin* the more she can see of her future life by dreaming.

If a girl fasts ten days it is supposed to cover the whole period of her life. During this time she does not only go without food, but also without water. It is during this time that she learns whether the *gichimanidoo* will accept her as a *mashkikiiwikwe*, a doctor or healer, and if he does she composes songs which she is to sing when she is accepted. I had omitted to say also, a young girl had to wear mittens on her hands and a cloth or hood on the head to cover her hair, as we believe that if a girl touched her hair with bare hands the growth would be stunted and remain short forever. A woman with short hair is a disgrace and an object of contempt among our people.

Anishinaabeg Men

When a young man reached manhood he selected the longest days in the year, which was generally late spring and wandered away from the village into the lonely forest and there he would proceed to build a *wadiswan*, a nest, in some tree and he would lie down and commence his *giigwishimowin*, fast, which usually lasted from five to ten days without food or water. During the fast he had many dreams, and by those dreams the course of his future life was guided, both on the war path and in hunting.

Tale of the Robin

A young man once wandered from his tribe in spring time to undergo the customary *giigwishimowin*. After he had fasted for several days his father came to him and advised him to fast as long as he could, which he obediently consented to do. He had fasted ten days when his father came to him and a second time urged him to prolong his fasting, notwithstanding the assertion of the young *anishinaabe* that he had foreseen the whole of his future life. The young man continued on his fast and when his father returned again he found his son reclining at the foot of the tree with his naked body painted red.

His first words to his father were these: *My father when you were here before I said that I had exhausted my giigwishimowin and had seen all I could of my future life.* While the young man was speaking his father saw him gradually raise from the ground. He seemed to fly slowly upwards until he reached some of the branches of the tree . . . He had become a robin with a red breast and said this to his father: *My father, whenever any danger threatens the anishinaabeg people I shall repeat these words in my song . . .*

nin-don-wan-chee-gay

nin-don-wan-chee-gay . . . signifying the
near presence of a foe or the approach of an
enemy, *as I am warning*, or *I am alarmed*. This
was the punishment the man received from the
gichimanidoo for compelling his son to fast too
long.

The *anishinaabeg* people until recent years,
looked upon the robin in the light of a guardian
manidoo, or spirit. This was more especially the
case when they were involved in wars with other
tribes. The *anishinaabeg* believed that if the
warning notes of the robin were heard in close
proximity to their camps, it was a signal that a
strong enemy was lurking near, and for them to
be on the alert or to break camp and hasten away
to some more favorable place. At other times
when there were *maji manidoog*, evil spirits, the
robin was believed to warn others of their
dangerous presence . . . I will relate an incident
handed to us by an old settler who was well
acquainted with the parties in question.

The venerable pioneer missionary, Father
Pierce, was once on a canoe journey up the
Mississippi accompanied by two *anishinaabeg*
men from Crow Wing. Some days after they had
proceeded on their journey, the priest missed his
purse which contained a few gold coins, medals,
crosses, and other trinkets. When he first missed

the purse he spoke not a word of his loss. After two or three days he came to the conclusion from the restless manner of one of his companions that he knew of the thief who had taken the purse. After reaching this conclusion he determined to try the efficacy of the warning cry of the robin on the first opportunity. When they had been striving for some time against a strong current, the notes of a chicakadee bird came clear and shrill to their ears, piping his notes as the *anishinaabeg* interpret them: *tchigibig . . . tchigibig . . .*

Do you hear that, said the priest, *that bird says go nearer the shore.* His companions answered *geget, geget*, sure, indeed, so they paddled the canoe nearer shore where the current not being so swift they soon ascended the rapids. This incident seemed to impress the *anishinaabe*. This was probably the more enhanced by the great deference in which the *makatewikwanaie* — the missionary dressed in black robes — are looked upon by the *anishinaabeg*. After ascending the rapids, they went ashore at a convenient landing, kindling an *ishkode* and prepared their noon day meal, after partaking of which, they reclined to enjoy the comforts of a smoke, and while they were engaged in this pleasant enjoyment they heard the sound *nin-don-wan-chee-gay* in the branches of the trees above their heads. Pointing in the

direction of the robin the priest addressed the
anishinaabe whom he mistrusted, *do you hear
that — do you understand what he says.* Without
once raising his gaze the *anishinaabe* answered,
geget.

Nothing more was said on the subject during
the day. Near sunset, they again pulled their
canoe ashore and after partaking of their supper,
retired for the night. Early the next morning the
anishinaabeg were astir and had breakfast
prepared before the priest had got up from his
rest. After the priest got up he kneeled down in
prayer and then went down to the river to bathe.
When he had returned to the camp he was
somewhat surprised to find the missing purse in
such a position that there could be no way for
him to miss seeing it. He took it up and
examined its contents — all was there. Thus the
superstition of the guilty party had made him
fearful that the robin having knowledge of the
theft would not rest until the *maji manidoog*,
evil spirits, were made known and punished.

Anishinaabeg Marriage

My grandchild, you want to know now about our marriage customs. Well, very many moons ago when my people wore no dress but that made from the furs and skins of animals slain in the chase, there were many very handsome women and men. A young man would say, *I am good looking. I don't think I could find a woman to suit me;* however, he would soon see some young woman who would impress him very much. He would then go on a hunt and select some fine furs and skins, which he would carry to the *wiigiwaam,* house, of the young girl to make her dresses to adorn her person, and if she accepted his attentions she would in return make him something whereby to adorn his person also, which was generally a handsome pair of *makizin,* moccasin. They were then betrothed to each other, and after this if everything was satisfactory with the parents of the young *anishinaabe* woman, she would then go in the neighborhood of her intended husband's home and cut *mitig,* wood, which she could carry on her back and take it to the *wiigiwaam,* house, of his parents. The wood was deposited at the entrance outside where she would await further developments. If there were no objections, his mother would come out and in a gentle manner would proceed to pinch or blow the nose of the young woman as a token that she was welcome as one of the family. Then, after the lapse of ten days from this time, the young couple would again meet together, and the man would take the hand of his bride and say *we must live for one another, we must be true and live together until we die.* They were then looked upon as man and wife.

Very often our men would take two and three wives and mostly of the same family, that is, sisters, as there were fewer family quarrels in this way. The best hunters always had the most wives. When a married man would see a woman whom he would fancy, he would pay his respects to her and if his attentions were favorably received, he would then consult the judgment of the other members of his family, and if there arose no objections the new applicant was brought home to the bosom of his family. If there were objections, the new bride would remain with her parents or an additional *wiigiwaam,* house, would be added to the much married possessions of the man. The wife which was first married generally ranks first in the family although the children of the different wives were looked upon with equal consideration by the father.

Another custom among my people and which

many of them practice to this day is, when a
man falls in love and would marry some young
woman, he takes his blanket and goes in the
neighborhood of her home, and awaits when all
have retired for the night and the camp fires
have burned low, when he proceeds to enter the
wiigiwaam, and having assured himself where
the young woman is reposing, which is generally
by the side of her mother, he quietly lies down
beside the young woman and if she accepts of his
courtship, they proceed to chat quietly during
the night — the lover taking his leave always
before sunrise. These visits are repeated several
times. If they concluded to get married, they
would allow the light of the sun to shine upon
them in the same couch in the *wiigiwaam* of her
parents. They had then sealed their vows and
become man and wife.

When there was any objections on the part of
the young woman, it was manifested by sitting
up on her couch while her mother would kindle
the smoldering embers into a blazing *ishkode*
This was an intimation to the young man that
he was not welcome and his absence desired. He
would then without further ceremony hasten
away. Sometimes when the parents of the young
woman did not approve of the young man, he
would resort to conciliatory measures by going
on a prolonged hunt and securing an amount of
deer and other game and some fine furs, and

taking the same would go and deposit it at the
entrance of the *wiigiwaam* of his lover and go to
his home. After repeating this two or three times
the parental obduracy would generally be
overcome. If not, and as a last resort, the mother
of the young *anishinaabe* man would go and
intercede in behalf of her son to the mother of
the young *anishinaabe* woman and happy results
would almost always follow this feminine
diplomacy.

My grandchild, you ask me if there was no
jealousy in those days. Well, it was as it is
today, only the spite was perhaps more bitter
and the revengeful feeling more severe than it is
now. It was no uncommon occurrence among
the women for a wife or rival crazed with love
and jealous frenzy to seek an early opportunity
to viciously attack the object of her hatred and if
possible cut off her nose or her braids of hairs —
the former object being to disfigure the face and
the latter to disgrace the victim. Among the men
death was often the result of rivalry in love
affairs.

Anishinaabeg Spirit

It may not be known to many of our readers that not many years ago there existed a class of individuals among the *anishinaabeg* who were known as *tchissakiwinini*, a person who knows spiritual magic, whose vocations and feats were similar to those of the eastern jugglers in such feats as the rope-tying, knife-swallowing and fire-eating tricks. These beings were looked upon as equal to the *mashkikiiwinini*, in many respects. In fact we may say that the representatives of the healing art were divided into four classes: *Mashkikiiwinini*, dreamers, blowers, and *tchissakiwinini*.

We will now speak of the *tchissakiwinini*. They were supposed to be leagued with the imaginary dwellers of the earth spirits and to hold communion with the different *manidoog*, spirits, who presided over the destiny of the dead and living worlds. Prominent among which was the *mechekans* — king of the turtles — who was regarded as a very powerful *manidoo* of good or evil, and who could converse with and look all over the world. Of course there were many other *manidoog* of minor power, but all were subject to the turtle. And the *mechekans* would communicate with the outside world through the *tchissakiwinini*, and when any person desired to know something about absent friends or relatives, or whether a sick person would overcome sickness and live, or whether death would follow, and where one would find some lost and stolen articles, as also a medium between the living and the dead to bring tidings from departed friends, they would repair to some *tchissakiwinini* and consult him about any subject they wished.

The mode of proceeding was generally in this wise: when anyone wished some favor of the *mechekans*, they would go and consult the *tchissakiwinini* taking some gift along, usually *asemaa*, tobacco, with which to please the *manidoo* and be deserving of the goodwill of all the other *manidoog* who may take part in the ceremony. If everything was favorable, the inquiring party would be informed and invited to come at a stated time and place, where the *tchissakiwinini* would have erected a *tchissakan*, which was built of stout poles eight to ten feet long driven firmly into the ground, and in such a manner as to form a circular body. These were attached at intervals on the inside to strong hoops and bound with thongs or some other stout cords, and over this on the outside was fastened *apakweshkway,* a cattail mat, so as to obscure the interior of the *tchissakan* from outside view. When the shades of evening were falling — this was the time that the inhabitants of the *manidoo* world were supposed to deign to hold communion with the living — the *tchissakiwinini* would seat himself with his guest or guests about a fire on the outside and all would join in a smoke, after which he would proceed to enter the *tchissakan* closing the opening after him, and ascend to the top, where he would sit for some time, singing and talking to the *manidoo,* while those on the outside would join in the song beating a drum at the same time. He would then descend, when immediately the *tchissakan* would become very much agitated and begin to sway while a great commotion and mumblings as of many voices could be heard proceeding from the interior and sounds would seem to come from round about the outside — the *tchissakiwinini* are masters of the art of ventriloquism.

At a given signal all would join in the exclamation of *ho ho ho, bendigan, bendigan. Mechekans* had arrived and was ready to listen to and answer any inquiries they had to make. After all questions had been answered, the party would deposit his or her gifts and take their departure, feeling satisfied that they had conversed with visitors or departed friends from the world of the *manidoog*, spirits.

Let it not be supposed that all the *anishinaabeg* were formerly believers in the *tchissakiwinini*, but like all other communities or races of men, they were divided in their faith and beliefs — religiously, socially, spiritually and regarding the healing arts. Skeptics were not uncommon amongst the *anishinaabeg*.

The largest denominations were to be found among the followers of the *midewiwin* and the *mashkikiiwinini*. The other denominations or followers of the *tchissakiwinini*, dreamers and blowers, were about equally divided, and in comparison to the adherents of spiritualism, faithcurers and clairvoyants, with the exception of the atheists, all believed in the existence and supremacy of a *gichimanidoo*, and also in the existence of a *majimanidoo*, evil spirits.

The *wandering ground* was supposed to be the place where the spirit of the departed had to abide at least one year as a restless wanderer, doing penance for past transgressions during life, and sometimes the spirit could find no rest until relieved by the *mashkikiiwinini*, who was kept informed of the condition of the *wanderer* by the supposed visitations of the *manidoo*, in his dreams. The *happy hunting ground*, of course, was looked upon as the *home of rest* — the abiding place of the just and worthy.

There was still another class who believed that between this life and the hereafter there coursed a *ziibi*, river, whose rapid waters was spanned by the bridge of *destiny*, where the spirit of the departed had to cross over in order to reach the *shining shores* of the *happy hunting grounds*. This bridge was supposed to be built of long limber poles and very shaky, and when a spirit was about to cross, it would become agitated to a degree equal to the sins the spirit was guilty of — for instance, if a spirit was worthy to enter the *happy hunting grounds*, he experienced no difficulty in crossing. On the other hand, if he were a *majimanidoo*, the bridge would become so agitated that the spirit would fall into the river, and being unable to rise, would continue falling indefinitely.

The *anishinaabe* leader *saycosegay* — a member of the *midewiwin* — told the following *dibaajimowin*, story or narrations of events, about the powers vested in the *tchissakiwinini* to inflict punishment upon those who were guilty of any misdeeds against other members of the tribe.

When I was a young man I had occasion to visit an *anishinaabe oodena*, town or village, on *puckagoma lake*. I was accompanied by my father and several other *anishinaabeg* people living near Mille Lac. In those days I indulged

considerably in *anishinaabe makizin ataage*,
moccasin game, and among other things I won
was a flintlock gun. It seemed however, that the
gun did not belong to the man from whom I had
won it, but to a powerful *tchissakiwinini* who
had loaned it to the man who lost it to me. After
a stay of several days at this *oodena*, town or
village, we started for home. About an hour after
our arrival at the first encampment which we
made after leaving the *oodena*, I kept hearing the
tingling of bells such as are used to ornament a
tchissakan. At the same time I began to feel a
dizzy sensation. I said to my companions, *do you
hear those bells, they seem to be a great distance
away yet I hear them distinctly.* My father
immediately said some *maji* would occur to me,
and that I should have painted my face *makade*,
black, before leaving the *oodena*, to guard against
majimanidoo. While my father was talking a
voice whispered a message to me . . . I was
invited to attend a *manidoo* council. I was very
reluctant about accepting this invitation, but
some invisible power seemed to control me.

I saw at a great distance an opening which
seemed brilliantly lighted, and I was directed to
go there. I travelled as fast as thought, and upon
my arrival there I found the opening to be the
top of a *tchissakan.* I entered and was kindly
greeted by the *manidoo.* They were not much
larger than *waawaatesiwag*, fireflies. There was

one however, who was larger than the rest and
with a very large head, whose eye glared at me
and seemed very much displeased with me.
Upon closer examination I found him to be the
tchissakiwinini whose gun I had won. Looking
about the *tchissakan* I recognized in the dark
several young men of the *oodena* which I had left
that day, and among them the man from whom I
had won the gun. I turned to the *tchissakiwinini*
and said: *my friend you are doing me a great
injustice by compelling me to attend this
meeting on account of your gun. I did not know
it was yours and I won it fairly. If I had stolen it
you might have had good reasons for endeavoring
to punish me.* All this time the *anishinaabeg*
people outside the *tchissakan* were clamoring for
my retention and urged my prosecution, but the
ikwe manidoo, woman spirit, was guarding me,
and she was attended by another *manidoo* who
was also friendly to me, and it so happened that
they were placed to guard the entrance at the top
of the *tchissakan* through which I meditated to
escape. When I was ready to attempt my escape,
I made a sign to my guardian and made a dash
for the opening and easily made my escape. My
spirit came back to my body, and when I
regained consciousness, I found myself
surrounded by *niikaanisag*, brothers or friends, to
whom I related my experience. It was a long
time before I got over the effects of my spiritual

adventure. Had it not been for the presence of my *ikwe manidoo*, I do not know what final punishment would have been inflicted upon me. I knew the moment I entered the *tchissakan*, that my *ikwe manidoo*, was present as I recognized her, having seen her in my dreams during my *giigwishimowin*, fast, which I underwent when I arrived at maturity or manhood. Had I taken the precautions to paint my face *makade*, black, before leaving the *oodena*, my *ikwe manidoo*, would in a dream have warned me of the impending danger which I could have averted.

Saycosegay further told about the custom of *giigwishimowin* which was for the purpose of guarding against *majimanidoog*, evil spirits. He believes that every *anishinaabe* has a guardian spirit. He also told that when he was a young man incidents similar to that which he related were of frequent occurrence, and that those who did not comply with the custom of *giigwishimowin* frequently became insane when attacked by the *manidoo*, controlled by the *tchissakiwinini*.

The Midewiwin

At the beginning of the big earth there existed on it only four persons — two men and two women — who had not the power to think, or to discriminate between right and wrong. The *gichimanidoo*, the great spirit, finally gave them the power to see, to think, and to learn the duties which have been imposed upon mankind. When they had acquired a knowledge of these duties the population of the earth began to increase, and the *anishinaabeg* people soon became quite numerous. It was at this time that the *gichimanidoo* observed that his grandchildren, the *anishinaabeg* people, were in deep distress. The *gichimanidoo* frequently saw the people crying — some of their numbers were being laid away in trees after being wrapped up in mats — and it became apparent to the *gichimanidoo* that this deep distress and sorrow was caused by disease and death which threatened to annihilate the *anishinaabeg* unless he made some provision for their salvation.

After considering for some time as to what would be best for the people the *gichimanidoo* called four of the leading *manidoog* from the different layers of the earth to consult with them. After the *gichimanidoo* had imparted to these *manidoo* his plans, he was at a loss in what manner to convey them to the *anishinaabeg* on the big earth.

His message was of too much importance to convey it to the people in their dreams. It was finally decided that the services of the *manidoo* of the *giizis*, sun or moon, should be called for this purpose. A message to this effect was sent to the *giizis*, in which he was directed to come on the big earth and to be conceived and born of a certain woman. In the course of time the child was born, and it was a boy. After this child had become several years of age he accompanied a hunting expedition. During this trip a child died in an *oodena* near by, and his parents, who were reluctant about laying his body away, resolved to take it back to their *oodena*. The son of the *giizis* was playing around an *ishkode*, fire, when his supposed father approached him and the child looking up said: *My father, I pity my people.* His father replied: *My son, we all pity them.*

The child spoke again saying: *My father, I shall give the child who is dead a new life.* His father rebuked him for saying this but the boy insisted that he would, if his directions were followed, bring the child to life. *My father,* he said, *you call all the old and wise men of the tribe and after you have erected a large lodge of sufficient size to accommodate them, place the*

body of the dead child in the center of the lodge.
You must be sure to build the lodge so that the
entrance will be facing the waaban, the east.
After you have done as I have directed, all the
men that will be inside the lodge must smoke
their pipes.

Having given these directions the boy
disappeared from the *oodena*, town or village.
His directions were followed implicitly. While
the wise men were sitting in the large lodge,
strange noises were heard in the direction of the
waabano, dreamer or healer, and the wise men
looking that way saw a *gichimakwa*, great bear,
approaching. When the *gichimakwa* had reached
the entrance of the lodge he assumed the form of
a boy. It was the boy who had directed the big
lodge to be built. Upon entering the lodge he ran
around to the left side of the lodge exclaiming,
whe,whe,whe,whe, at every step. In his hands he
held a *mashkiki*, medicine pouch and when he
had made a complete circle of the lodge he
stopped and making a motion towards the body
of the dead child with the *mashkiki* pouch
which he held in his hands he exclaimed, *whay,*
ho, ho,ho. The body of the child quivered and
after this had been repeated the fourth time the
dead child came to life. The boy then took the
child in his arms and placed him in those of his
own father, saying: *My father, give this child to*
his parents.

Then the boy said: *My friends. I am not one of you. I am the giizis manidoo,* sun spirit. *I was sent to teach you how to attain a new life when you are about to lose one. This man is not my father. I am a manidoo and can take any form I wish, I came on earth to teach you what I was sent among you for.*

He then explained the *midewiwin* and gave *the people* new life. Then he disappeared. This is how my *anishinaabeg* ancestors told me the *midewiwin* was handed to *the people.*

Midewiwin Initiation

Whenever any person was desirous of joining the *midewiwin* his application was usually submitted to a *midewiwin* leader accompanied with *asemaa*, tobacco, and other articles of value. Three other leaders were then called and together they smoked and discussed the merits and virtues of the applicant, necessary to warrant his initiation to the sacred rites of the *midewiwin*. If this meeting resulted favorably to the applicant, a day was set on which to perform the solemn rights of the initiation, and the applicant,was notified of this decision and instructed to prepare him or herself for the ceremony which duties were to compose a recitation and rehearsal of chants after the instructions of a *midewiwin* leader appointed for this occasion. These rehearsals are continued for about a week previous to admission of an applicant in the presence of the leader and other worthies of the *midewiwin*.

On the sixth day, all parties interested, including the applicant, proceed to the scene selected to solemnize the ceremony where a *midewigaan*, *midewiwin* lodge, had been built. This lodge is usually seventy-five to one hundred feet in length, fifteen to twenty feet in width and

five to six feet high, covered over with boughs
and *apakweshway*, cattail mat. Poles are
suspended across the interior whereon is laid the
goods and other articles offered by the applicant
for initiation and other parties who may be
seeking favors from the *gichimanidoo* at the
hands of his agents, the leaders of the
midewiwin. A cedar post is planted about two-
thirds of the way from the entrance to the other
end of the *midewigaan*. On the top of this post
the figure of a bird, resembling a dove, is placed
looking towards the ground where a mat is
placed . . . whereon the applicant for initiation is
to seat himself. A rock is placed midway
between this post and the further end of the
lodge and between this rock and post is placed
the mat under the vigil of the bird which is
perched on the post. As soon as the four
midewiwin leaders enter the *midewigaan*, they
take up the *mitigwakik*, *mide* drum, and in
unison commence to beat on it, while the
leaders chant *midewiwin* songs. The *mitigwakik*
is covered with a head of raw deer hide, and
when it is beat upon, it produces a weird and
hollow sound which can be heard miles away.

After the leaders each sing a song, one leader
takes a *mide miigis*, mide sacred shell, the
emblem of the *midewiwin*, and holds it in the
palm of the left hand with a *mashkiki* pouch in
the right hand. This pouch is made from the

skin of a weasel or other small animals and not unusually the skin of a human hand. Instances are related where the hide of young children were made to answer the purposes. The *midewiwin* leader proceeds to circle to the left uttering at every step the exclamation, *whe,whe,whe,* until he reaches a certain spot near the entrance of the lodge, where he stops and turning to the person undergoing initiation he addresses him or her thus: *whay, ho,ho,ho,ho,niijii,niijii,niijikiwe.* This means, *welcome, welcome, my friend, my brother.*

The leaders then walk and assemble together at the rear end of the *midewigaan,* and converse in a language which none but members high in the *midewiwin* can understand, and those to whom it has been explained. The translation is as follows:

After the gichimanidoo had made known to his children, the anishinaabeg, how to obtain a new life, he asked, what must I do for the people. They are empty-handed. He closed his hands and then opened them and there was the great miigis. This great striped otter then was selected to distribute the miigis. The gichimanidoo taking a large sea shell said to the otter, you shall have this for a lodge, which means the midewigaan — the sacred lodge of the midewiwin. The striped otter was not an otter but a *manidoo* who took the form of any animal

it desired. His name was *swangideeshkawed* and
four *manidoog* guarded and waited on him. He
summoned these four *manidoog* to him and
addressing them said: *Go and tell the leaders of
the midewiwin manidoog I have something to
say to them, and from the giiwedin, north;
zhaawans, south; waaban, east; and
bangishimog, west, the midewiwin manidoog
were summoned to appear before
swangideeshkawed.*

When they had assembled, he said to them,
*Go on the big earth and distribute for the use of
my children, the manidoowish, that they may
use their skins for mashkiki pouches.* After the
swangideeshkawed had given directions to the
four *midewiwin manidoog*, he assumed the
shape of an otter and covered his body with the
miigis.

While the old men were sitting in the
midewigaan which had been built by the
directions of the *giizis manidoo*, they heard
curious noises as if somebody was laughing —
the noise being similar to that which you have
probably heard made by an otter. Upon looking
up they saw the *gichi miigis* when it first came
over from the big earth. It is believed to have
first come ashore at the mouth of *monayah ziibi*
— St. Lawrence seaway — where for many days
the rays of the sun reflected on the back of the
miigis over the earth imparting new life to the

anishinaabeg people.

From thence he disappeared and at intervals he appeared along the shores of the seaway until he reached the great chain of lakes. The *gichi miigis*, the great sacred shell, finally reached the shining shores of *sagidawidjiwan* — *anishinaabe gichigami* — *two miles from where Bayfield now stands at a place known as makade ziibi*, black river. Here the *gichi miigis* came ashore to rest. At last he reached a place known as *mooningwanekaning*, where while resting, the *gichi miigis* saw the smoke of many *ishkode* and he soon ascertained that a great *oodena* was situated here and that many thousand people lived there. Here he resolved to deliver the message of the *gichimanidoo* to the *anishinaabeg* people.

At Sandy river there is an open spot, which looks like a prairie from a distance, and it was here where the old and wise *anishinaabeg* men of the tribe had built a *midewigaan*. When the *gichi miigis* observed this and being a part of his mission, he proceeded to enter and abide there for some time, teaching the wise men further into the mysteries of the *midewiwin* and of the medicinal virtues of roots and herbs. The entrance of the *midewigaan* was guarded by *majimanidoo*, an evil spirit, who would not allow anyone to pass. The *miigis* directed the

mashikikiiwinini to kill and cook an *animosh*, a
dog, as a peace offering, which would please the
majimanidoo and no one would be molested who
wished to enter.

When you enter a *midewigaan* the first thing
you observe is a painted cedar post some
distance from the entrance, and near the
entrance is a large stone. Midway between this
stone and post the *gichi miigis* is believed to
take his place during the solemn celebration of
the different rites of the *midewiwin*. All
sacrifices and offerings are directed there. The
stone is believed to have the properties of
drawing disease from the body of a sick person,
and the post represents a tree which is an
emblem of life and strength, and so it is that a
sick person undergoing treatment at the hands of
members of the *midewiwin* is placed so as to
lean against this post.

The earth was bare when the *gichimanidoo*
first thought of the *midewiwin* as the trees and
stones and everything that grows was in the
second layer of the earth. When the stones and
trees heard the *manidoo* conversing about the
future of the *anishinaabeg*, they revolved to
appear on earth and after four trials they
succeeded in doing so. Since then they have
scattered everywhere.

Swangideeshkawed placed the *midewiwin*

manidoo at each of the four layers of the earth,
hence a person to avail him or herself of the
favors of all the leaders of the *midewiwin* must
therefore take four degrees in the *midewiwin*.

Birth of Naanabozho

A great many winters since when this country was occupied and owned exclusively by the *anishinaabeg* and other tribal peoples there lived on the shores of a large lake, in the *anishinaabeg* woodland country, with his band, a powerful but unprincipled chief, who had a son who besides being as unprincipled as his father, was a profligate and despised by his people.

In the same *oodena* there lived a widow with a daughter who was a virgin pure and beautiful, with whom the chief's son was infatuated, but whose advances were repulsed by the maiden. Finally, tiring of the repeated failures of his suit, he decided to rely on his prerogative as the son of a chief, by having a wife selected by his father whose requests or commands would have to be obeyed by the parents or guardians of any *anishinaabeg* in the band in the selection of a wife for the son. He informed his father of his desire to secure as his wife the girl in question. In due time the chief sent the customary presents to her mother with a demand for her daughter as a wife for his son, but the widow refused this, and with her daughter made her escape from the *oodena*.

After traveling five days and five nights

without camping, they arrived at a beautiful lake
where the widow decided to build a *wiigiwaam*
and live permanently. For some unaccountable
reason, the *manidoo* ignored and excluded the
presence of man from this vicinity, which
seemed to have been the meeting grounds of the
four powerful *manidoog* representing the four
winds.

One day while the young girl was gathering
manoomin, wild rice, the *giiwedin manidoo*,
north spirit, who chanced to be passing by spied
her and became very much enamored of her.
When she returned home she related to her
mother what she had observed. The latter
became very much alarmed and warned her
daughter to be very neat about her dress and
person, and to guard against the wiles of the
giiwedin, north, who was a very harsh fellow
and might carry her off. Some days after this the
young girl went into the woods to gather
blueberries that grew in abundance along the
banks of a brook which ran through a beautiful
grove of pine trees.

While she was busily engaged gathering
berries, the *giiwedin manidoo* in a very noisy
and boisterous manner, came to her, took her in
his arms and kissed her, fluttered her garments
and then departed from whence he had come.
For some time the young girl was overcome with
a delicious feeling of joy and happiness and she

reclined to rest.

When she awoke from this delicious stupor,
every tree in the forest were mingling their
voices with the birds in piping forth their
sweetest songs. When she had returned home,
she related to her mother what had taken place.
Her mother listened to this in silence and when
the young girl had concluded, said: *My daughter
this was foreordained.*

The young girl knew she had conceived and
would become a mother. In the course of time
the young girl became very sick and for several
days she lay in pain on a couch of boughs.

One day feeling a little better than usual, she
went outside and laid down beneath the shade of
a balsam tree. While resting thus she heard
voices talking as if they were in dispute, and at
the same time the sweet tones of a nightingale
were heard, as if endeavoring to pacify the
disputants. Suddenly there was a rustle, and a
great gust of wind from the north swept by and
taking the young girl in his embrace disappeared
from the earth. The girl's mother who had been
enjoying a nap was awakened by the commotion,
looked about the *wiigiwaam* for her daughter,
and being satisfied she was not within, hurried
outside searching and calling for her beloved
child, but the sweet tones of the nightingale
were the only sounds that answered her call. At
last, worn and with grief and weeping, she

returned to her now lonely *wiigiwaam,* and while passing the tree under which her daughter had so lately reclined, she overheard a wee little voice say : *nookomis, grandmother, do not cry. I am your grandchild and have been left here to comfort and to take care of you. My name is naanabozho and I shall do many things for the comfort of you and my people and when my work is done, I will take you home to your daughter, my mother, where you will never be parted from her again.*

Naanabozho Obtains Fire

About one of the first things *naanabozho*
talked about with *nookomis*, was the absence of
ishkode, as the nights at that time of the year
were very chilly, and the family inheritance of
skins and furs was somewhat limited.

One morning having slept colder than usual,
he said, *nookomis, it is very cold here at night. I
wish we had ishkode to warm ourselves.
Nookomis said, nia, my grandchild, I don't think
we can get ishkode as it is a long distance across
anishinaabe gichigami to the island home of
giizis manidoo, sun spirit, where ishkode can be
found, and then too, a person would have to go
before one of his smiles — rays — but that has
never been done for the island and the sacred
lodge of giizis manidoo is strongly guarded by
many manidoog and his only companions are his
daughters — the clouds — who weep rain for
him when he is angry or when his heart feels
bad.*

*No, my grandchild, I would not advise you to
undertake such a long journey and so hazardous
a task.* But nothing daunted *naanabozho*. He was
young and ambitious and already he was feeling
the thirst for glory and the achievements of great
deeds and he at once set about laying plans for

the undertaking. He went himself to the woods
where he held a council with the trees of the
forest — this was presumably the first council or
secret session ever held — finally ending with
the birch trees consenting to give some of the
wiigwass, birchbark, which was part of their
snow white garments and lined with rich purple
and gold. The majestic cedar tendered him a few
fragrant splinters for the keel and ribs of his
craft. The stately tamarac donated some roots to
lace together, and the princely pine tree assured
him that it would shed a few tears of pitch to
cement the whole together and make it
waterproof.

In time the keel was laid. The light, feathery
ribs were put in place and the white and gold
colored robes of the queen of the forest was
gracefully set about the corset and the root was
made to gently clasp and lace them together
while the tears of pitch smoothed the creases.
Thus, the first *wiigwaasi jiimaan*, birchbark
canoe, was finished. None but *naanabozho* and
his descendants have ever succeeded in building
a *wiigwaasi jiimaan* to such perfection.

When all was ready, *naanabozho* embraced
nookomis and bid her an affectionate goodbye,
after having instructed her to prepare an earthern
pot wherein she was to place some punk
procured for the purpose, and watch for his
coming. He embarked in his birchbark canoe and

having summoned the aid of his father, the north
wind, and his uncles, the south and east
winds,and the west wind spirit, he was soon
gone and out of sight.

At daybreak the next morning he found
himself near the glittering shores of the *manidoo*
island home. He hastily stepped ashore and after
concealing his birchbark canoe, sat down a
moment to determine what course was best to
pursue to procure *ishkode*. *Naanabozho* had the
power to assume the shape of almost any animal
he desired so he changed himself into a rabbit
and he proceeded to drench himself with water
and sand, then he lay himself down close to the
edge of the water apparently more dead than
alive. Presently two pretty daughters of the *giizis
manidoo* came to the beach to draw water with
which to shower life with the crystal beads of
the morning dew. One of them saw the poor,
forlorn looking rabbit and she called her sister's
attention to the pitiable object. They could not
tell what it was, having never seen anything like
it before, however, their hearts were touched
with pity and they concluded to take it home to
their *wiigiwaam* and beg their father, the *giizis
manidoo*, to smile on the poor half-drowned
creature so that it might get warmed and
revived.

When they got home, the *giizis manidoo*, was
already awake and everything was warm and

pleasant inside of the sacred lodge. No question was asked by the *manidoog* guarding the entrance as they were subject to the daughters as well as to the *giizis manidoo*. So they passed in unmolested and tenderly laid down their burden and went about their work.

Soon the rabbit began to show signs of life by jumping up and skipping about the lodge at a very lively rate and greatly to the amusement of the two daughters. This soon attracted the attention of their father, the *giizis manidoo*, and he asked his daughters what this was that they had brought into the lodge while rebuking them for admitting strangers in his presence without first asking his permission. While this conversation was going on, the rabbit had come and sat down opposite the *giizis manidoo* within easy exit of the door. There he sat in the most matter of fact way moving his long ears to and fro and twitching his lips and nose in a most amusing and ridiculous fashion. While in this position, the *giizis manidoo* happened to look at him and so comical did the rabbit seem, that he could not restrain a smile of merriment escaping him. The glittering rays of the smile from the *giizis manidoo* rested between the shoulders of the rabbit. As soon as this had taken place, *naanabozho* — for he was the rabbit — caught sparks from the fiery ray smile on a small piece of punk he had fastened between his shoulders

and darted out of the lodge and sped like an
arrow from a bow towards where his birchbark
canoe lay concealed. In less time than it takes to
write this, he was off and far away on his return
voyage homeward.

When the *giizis manidoo* discovered what had
been done he hid his face and bid his daughters,
the clouds, forthwith to weep rain, endeavoring
to quench the spark of *ishkode* that *naanabozho*
had stolen. But so swift did the *noodin manidoo*,
wind spirit, hurry his light craft before them,
that it was found impossible to overtake him.
And thus he was allowed to proceed the rest of
his voyage unmolested.

The swiftness of *naanabozho* and his craft
caused the burning punk to be fanned into a
blaze and before he could extricate himself from
his rabbit skin, the hair was afire, and matters
looked serious sure enough. He was now nearing
the shore from whence he came, and he at once
commenced to howl and called loudly for
nookomis to hurry up: *Come to me, I am afire,
hi-hai, nookomis come quick!*

When *nookomis* heard this, she rushed out of
her *wiigiwaam* and hurried towards the shore
carrying with her the pot she had prepared. So
excited was she that she forgot all about her
stick and a sprained ankle. When she reached the
shore and pulled the birchbark canoe on the
beach she first shook some of the *ishkode* into

the pot then she proceeded to try and relieve
naanabozho from his agonizing predicament. In
many places the rabbit skin had burned through.
And when at last *nookomis* pulled it off his
back, great pieces of his own skin and flesh came
off with it.

Poor *naanabozho*, he was indeed a sorry-
looking sight after he was relieved of his fiery
jacket. *Nookomis* tenderly supported him to
reach the *wiigiwaam* where she prepared a soft
couch of moss and leaves, and upon which he
lay down. The *nookomis* turned her attention to
the *ishkode* in the pot. She went out and brought
in some dry faggot, as she had been instructed to
do, and soon a bright *ishkode* was shedding its
grateful warmth about the *wiigiwaam.* This
pleased *naanabozho* exceedingly and he felt that
the great comfort *ishkode* would be to him and
his brothers in the future, would more than
repay him for the terrible ordeal he had just
undergone.

Then he asked *nookomis* to go to a certain
place and bring some clay and dirt with which to
dress his wounds. He also instructed her to
gather certain kinds of roots and herbs for the
same purpose, which were to be used by his
brothers likewise whenever they had need of
them thereafter. After his wounds had been
dressed he partook of some herb tea and then lay
down to rest. Worn, weary and sore, he soon was

in a sound sleep. Then the spirit of *naanabozho* wafted to the most enchanting scenes, the wonderous marvels and glories in the realms of dreamland, to get more instruction regarding the improvements of this earth.

Naanabozho and Nookomis

When *naanabozho* awoke from his peaceful slumbers, he refreshed himself with a hearty breakfast, and then he caused a wind to blow from the north in the direction of the *anishinaabeg oodena* from whence his grandmother and her daughter — his mother — had come, and he said *nookomis: I am going to send ishkode to all my relatives who live in the country where you and my mother come from.*

Nookomis has never told *naanabozho* of his origin and she was continually in dread lest he would seek to know more of his ancestors, and whenever he spoke of the *oodena*, she would become very much alarmed. One day it was decided to move to the outlet of a big lake, and when they had selected a convenient location, *naanabozho* instructed *nookomis* to go and prepare poles and birchbark with which to build a *wiigiwaam*. When the *wiigiwaam* was completed and they had moved and got settled down, *naanabozho* arranged to go on an *amik*, beaver, hunt: There were a great many *amikwag* in those days and it was not long before he had secured a good supply which was brought home to the *wiigiwaam*. *Nookomis* was instructed how to prepare the pelts and make them into nice comfortable blankets, such as the *anishinaabeg* used before the *gichi mookomaanag*, white people, came into the country.

One day when *naanabozho* had enjoyed the pleasure of a hearty meal of beaver tail, and lay in comfort on his couch of skins and boughs he asked *nookomis* to relate the history of his ancestors and his father and mother. *Nookomis* endeavored to evade answering his questions, but *naanabozho* seemed so determined to know that she finally answered him in this wise way: *Your mother was a very beautiful girl who had many suitors, but the ogimaa, the chief, of the tribe*

*desired that the youngest of his three sons
should marry her. I opposed this marriage
because the young man was indolent, lazy and
good for nothing. The ogimaa sent four requests
for the hand of my daughter — your mother —
but I firmly refused to listen to his proposition.
When he found that I would not consent to my
daughter's marriage with his son, he called in
one of his counsellors and after a private
conference the latter advised the chief to cause
me to be assassinated, that by doing this the
only obstacle to his son's marriage with my
daughter, would be removed. A friend of mine
overheard this plot and immediately informed
me of it. That day I prepared for a journey and
left the oodena with your mother at night, and
after a weary journey of many days we camped
by the lake where you were born.*

*When the ogimaa heard of our flight, he was
terribly enraged and forthwith dispatched runners
in all directions to endeavor to overtake and
bring us back to the oodena, the chief himself
joining in the pursuit. This pursuit was kept up
for four days, when the ogimaa ordered a halt to
counsel with his tchissakiwinini, but the
manidoo who favored our flight refused to give
them any information.*

*We had lived on the shore of the lake for
many moons when one night, I was warned in a
dream not to allow your mother to stand on her*

*feet for seven days and not to face the wind
during that time. This was during the blueberry
season and I guarded her very closely after that
in order that she would not stand up. One day,
however, while we were picking blueberries I
had occasion to leave her for a short time.
During my absence she spied a large bunch of
blueberries in a marsh and it being too wet to
crawl towards them she thought there would be
no harm in walking to the berries, but the
moment she stood up, the giiwedin, north, who
had been lurking in the vicinity came and
embraced her. When this had occurred, she fell
prostrated on the ground. I ran to her and when
she again opened her eyes, she, as well as
myself, knew that she had conceived. And after
you were born, she went down into the clear
water of the lake to bathe and was there attacked
and swallowed up by the missameg.*

Nookomis knew she had been telling a
falsehood but she was afraid that if she related
the truthful history of the birth of naanabozho,
the sad abduction of his mother and of her being
borne to her far away island home, he would get
injured if he endeavored to fight the *manidoo*
who had caused all this to come about, and
which had left him an orphan in the world.

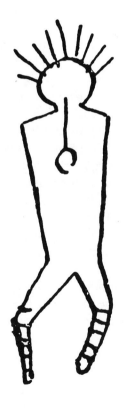

Naanabozho and Missameg

After the conclusion of the narrative of *nookomis*, *naanabozho* pondered long and silently. Finally he requested *nookomis* to go and prepare him a *tchissakan* as he wished to invoke the *manidoo* to give him information and power as to where he would find and destroy the *missameg*. After he had completed that solemn occasion he came out and informed *nookomis* of his purpose and to prepare him for his journey. *Naanabozho* said: *I will be gone four days, on the fourth day if all goes well with me, I will be on the shore of that bay where the wind ceases to breathe. You will know this by the skies which will appear red and smiling, and should I have trouble and not reach there the skies will be very dark and cloudy.* He then painted his face black and embarked into his birchbark canoe and started in search of the *missameg*, the whale. After wandering about for two or three days, he concluded, as the *manidoo* had told him, that he was near where the *missameg* lived and as he had been instructed, commenced to sing *missameg, hay,hay, be nah we co she shin — whale come swallow me.*

Missameg, the whale, heard this singing and it annoyed him very much. He said that

naanabozho was too filthy for him to swallow,
so he directed a large pickerel to go and swallow
the filthy morsel. When the pickerel appeared,
he was hailed by *naanabozho* with *ishnee cheem,
keen e-nah, — my little brother, it is you —*
meaning the whale, but the answer he received
was *No, I am only a pickerel and came to obey
the command of missameg who got tired of your
song.*

When *naanabozho* heard this he became very
angry and said to the pickerel, *Go back, you are
not the one who killed my mother.* The pickerel
returned and related to the whale what
naanabozho had said. This provoked *missameg*
and as the taunting song of the former kept
ringing in his ear, he was determined to go
himself and make a meal out of the filthy
intruder.

The father of *missameg* remonstrated against
his resolution by saying that *naanabozho* coming
amongst them with his invitation to be
swallowed up boded no good, and it was best to
leave him alone. But *missameg* was in such a
rage he would listen to no further argument but
went forthwith and swallowed *naanabozho,*
birchbark canoe and all.

When the *missameg* had swallowed
naanabozho he felt very sick and he soon became
insensible. When he had revived a little, he felt
that he must have swallowed all the disagreeable

things in the world. He also heard *naanabozho* soliloquizing to himself in this wise: *It is true that I have been swallowed . . . fool . . . he shall now suffer for having swallowed my mother and making me an orphan.*

Then *naanabozho* commenced to take note of his surroundings and the first thing he saw was a weasel, who like himself, had been swallowed by the whale. Then his eyes rested on a large object above him which seemed to keep up a constant fluttering motion. As *naanabozho* could not reach up, and being anxious to know more of his surroundings, he inquired of the weasel what the object was and the weasel informed him that it was the heart of the *missameg*. With this intelligence *naanabozho* was greatly please, because he thought the whale was very foolish to keep his heart in such an exposed position. Then *naanabozho* addressing the weasel said: *We must destroy missameg or we, ourselves, will both die. If you will go up there and fight his heart and help me destroy him I will reward you by making you white in winter and brown in summer so that you can better avoid your enemies. I will also show you where to strike your enemy so that you can always draw blood from his heart.* The weasel attacked the heart of *missameg* vigorously. *Missameg* commenced at once to complain of being sick at the stomach and he attributed the disorder to indigestion caused by the unsavory mess he had lately swallowed.

The father of *missameg* said: *I told you naanabozho was destined to conquer all of us and he will surely kill you. Try and swallow enough water so as to drown him. Missameg* proceeded to do as he was bid but it was of no avail, as *naanabozho* could float about in his birchbark canoe despite all the water his enemy could swallow. When the whale could swallow no more water, he cried out in agony: *I cannot help myself; he is killing me.*

His father again spoke to him and said: *Go at once to the shore and endeavor to throw him up for should you remain here, he will surely kill you and then come out and kill the rest of us. Missameg* needed no second invitation to act on any suggestion which presented itself, looking to a relief from the terribly nauseous morsel which he had so imprudently swallowed. He forthwith started for the shore and in the direction of the home of *naanabozho.*

When *naanabozho* learned this he said to the weasel: *We will not injure him now until we reach the shore near our home.* After the whale had reached the shore he again proceeded to swallow water for the purpose of drowning *naanabozho* and then throwing him up. But at this time the weasel was busing biting and lacerating his heartstrings. *Missameg* soon ceased

all efforts and in a little while, after a few
convulsive flutters, lay still and dead.

On the fourth day after the departure of
naanabozho, nookomis arose early in the
morning and gazed eagerly at that portion of the
skies indicated to her by *naanabozho* previous to
his departure, and behold, it was bright and red.
And then she knew that all was well with her
grandchild. As instructed she started in the
direction of the shore. Here she was amazed to
see a monster fish apparently dead and floating
near the beach. Approaching nearer she was
surprised and terrified to hear the sound of voices
from within the big fish. Her fears were dispelled
when she heard a well-known voice calling and
instructing her to come and cut *missameg* open.
Nookomis did as she was bid and soon
naanabozho and his companion, the weasel,
came forth apparently none the worse from their
late experience in the bowels of *missameg*.

Return of Naanabozho

After his release, *naanabozho* accompanied by
nookomis, proceeded to their *wiigiwaam*. And
while he lay down to rest and sleep, *nookomis*
prepared a feast of ducks and *manoomin*, wild
rice. When the meal was ready, *naanabozho* was
awakened. He ate very heartily being very
hungry, as he had eaten nothing for four days.
He ate and rested at intervals until he had
consumed the whole of the ducks and
manoomin that *nookomis* had prepared. He then
informed *nookomis* that he wished her to join
him in a grand dance. A place was accordingly
arranged, a long lodge was built. This was
partially covered with boughs of balsam and
cedar and on the ground within were spread mats
and furs. *Naanabozho* had made extensive
preparations as he had extended a general
invitation to all of his *anishinaabe* relatives to be
present at the feast. But when the time had
arrived to commence the exercises, *nookomis*
and himself were the only beings present. This
did not seem to dishearten them in the least and
they danced and feasted and had a very merry
time, indeed. Then *naanabozho* made a speech
and in the heat of his discourse, he charged
nookomis with deceiving him with regard to his

birth and parents, and accused her of having
caused the death of his mother. At this period
naanabozho was very much excited and with
flashing eyes he turned to *nookomis* and
demanded that she tell him, under penalty of
death, the cause of his mother's death and all
she knew concerning his parents. *Nookomis*
though fearful of losing her life, endeavored to
pacify *naanabozho* and dissuade him from his
purpose of learning more of his past and
parentage. But no argument could turn him from
his purpose.

Finally, *nookomis* in a clear, calm voice spoke
to him thus: *My grandchild, you know not what
you ask. You should not let the pains and
disappointments of the past cloud the sunshine
of the present. The manidoog are powerful and
they know best what is for our good and it is not
right that we should seek to know what he
desires to keep from us. Were we permitted to
forsee the hidden paths of life, our hearts would
ever be in pain and our eyes ever bathed in tears.
You should, therefore, be satisfied that you have
been spared and are strong in body and mind,
and that some day you may be permitted to see
and live with your mother.*

Still *naanabozho* was obdurate and insisted
that *nookomis* should tell him what she knew
about his mother and father and the old woman
seeing that further dissuasion was useless,

addressed him thus: *My grandchild, you
yourself, killed your dear, beautiful mother. She
gave her sweet life that yours might be spared;
like the peaceful calm of dawn drawing aside the
curtains of eve before the advent of a new day;
like the lily that buds and blooms and feasts on
the ambrosial of its fragrance. It is life — a smile
— meekly given to the sunshine of another. Thus
it had to be, the manidoo had spoken in my
dreams that a virgin should be sacrified that
naanabozho should live, and that virgin was my
daughter — your mother.*

*You also were the cause of the death of your
brother, biwanag, as there were two of you —
twins. Your brother's spirit returned to the
fourth portion of the earth as a manidoo of
peace. As to your father, I fear to tell you, as he
is a powerful manidoo for good or evil and lives
in the fourth folds of the skies.*

The *manidoo* knew that his grandchild
naanabozho, was angry and he became very
much alarmed and he proceeded to call a council
to discuss the probable visit of *naanabozho* to his
realms, as it was supposed that his intended visit
was for the purpose of avenging his mother's
death. And it was known that he suspected his
father of being the cause, indirectly, of the death
of his mother.

Naanabozho and his Father

Naanabozho made extensive preparations to go
on the war path. He painted himself as no
anishinaabe ever was painted, and arming
himself with a war club, he started for the fourth
fold of the skies. The *manidoo* saw his
grandchild coming while he was yet in council
and he became very much alarmed as
naanabozho was invincible to the *manidoo* as
well as the living, so it was hurriedly decided
that he must endeavor to appease the anger of
his grandchild by offering and granting him the
full control of the earth, as sovereign lord and
master. So when *naanabozho*, who was in the
shape of a black cloud, came in sight several
manidoog tried to persuade him in order to talk
and reason with him so that he would not harm
his father, but their appeals were of no avail. In
blind frenzy *naanabozho* rushed at his father,
who calmly stood, erect and firm with arms
folded across his massive chest, and his snowy
locks trailing to the ground.

When *naanabozho* came near, he raised one of
his hands and motioned for him to stop. Then in
a deep, full voice he spoke thus: *My beloved son,
why do you seek to kill me. I did not kill your
mother. I loved her too well to do that, but your*

dear mother died that you might live. You,
whom I have guarded so fondly from infancy,
and now you seek and would kill me.

Again *naanabozho* was obdurate and raising
his war club on high would have struck his
father down, but suddenly there appeared before
him a beautiful vision, as of a young man with
eyes that seemed overflowing with mercy and
kindness and who seemed to look through and
through *naanabozho*. Then the vision spoke and
said: *Listen my brother, let not your hand be*
raised against another. Seek not to take away or
destroy that which you cannot give. Be
reconciled, the earth is given you control, now
peace be with you.

Naanabozho knew that this was the *manidoo*
of peace, his brother. So he allowed his father to
go unmolested while he went about consulting
the many *manidoog* as to the best course he
should pursue in assuming charge and control of
the earth. After he had learned what he desired
to know, he returned to *nookomis* and with the
avowed purposed of making a tour of the earth.

After *naanabozho* had returned to *nookomis*
and had refreshed himself with the soothing
comforts of sleep and food, he related to her the
incidents attendant on his journey, and of the
authority vested in him. He concluded by
informing *nookomis* of his intention of making
an extended tour of his realm, which would

occupy about two years. When *nookomis* learned this, she was much grieved.

My grandchild, the land which you intend to visit is infested with majimanidoo, evil spirits, principally the followers of wiindigoo, the cannibal, who are very numerous, powerful and ferocious. And no one who has ever got within their power has ever been known to return. They first charm their victims by the sweetness of their songs, then they strangle and devour them. But your principal enemy will be the gichi nita ataaged, the great gambler, who has never been beaten and who lives beyond the realm of the niibaa giizis, darkness, and near the shores of the happy hunting-ground. I would beseech you, therefore, not to undertake so dangerous a journey.

With the increasing laurels of conquest, *naanabozho* felt that he was brave and as such, should know no fear. The warning words of *nookomis* were unheeded. After having made all necessary preparations he bid *nookomis* goodbye and started on his journey. He followed the trail which led to the realms of *niibaa giizis* where all was shrouded in total darkness. Here he stopped and meditated as to what was best to be done. He consulted with the different birds and animals and friendly *manidoog*, and it was finally decided that *gookooko oo*, the owl, would lend him his eyes, and that *waawaatesi*, the

firefly, should also accompany him to light the
way. They were soon on their way through the
realms of *niibaa giizis*. All around was darkness
and *naanabozho*, in spite of his great owl eyes,
could discern nothing for some time but the
flitting of *waawaatesi*. For the first time in his
life he experienced the chilly breath of fear, and
wished that he had listened to the counsel of
nookomis. But just then a voice whispered in his
ear saying: *I am with you. You should never
fear.* At this his fears were dispelled and he
boldly walked on.

The path which *naanabozho* was traveling led
him through swamps and over high mountains
and by yawning chasms sometimes on the very
verge of some awful precipice, and then again
near the thundering roaring and maddening rush
of some furious stream or cataract. From pit and
chasm he saw the hideous stare of a thousand
gleaming eyes. He heard the groans, the hisses
and yells of countless fiends gloating over their
many victims — the victims of sin and shame.
Then *naanabozho* knew that this was the place
where the *great gambler* consigned the spirits of
his many victims and he vowed that if he ever
destroyed the *gichi nita ataaged*, he would
liberate the victims who were being tortured.

At last all noises gradually ceased, darkness
disappeared, and it was again sunlight.
Naanabozho put off his owl eyes and bid

waawaatesi to return from whence he had come. He then proceeded to a high eminence where he looked about for the *wiigiwaam* of the great gambler and he saw in the distance a large *wiigiwaam*. When he was very near the *wiigiwaam*, he saw that there were numerous trails coming from different directions but all leading towards the *wiigiwaam*. This *wiigiwaam* presented a ghastly and hideous appearance, it being completely covered with human scalps.

Naanabozho and the Gambler

Naanabozho approached the entrance of this
ghastly abode and raising the mat of scalps,
which served for a door, found himself in the
presence of the great gambler. He was a curious
looking being and seemed almost round in shape
and *naanabozho* thought he could not be a very
dexterous gambler who would let himself be
beaten by the being who was then grinning at
him. Finally the great gambler spoke and said:
*So, you too, have come to try your luck. And
you think I am not a very expert gambler.* He
grinned and chuckled — a horrible mingling of
scorn and ridicule.

Reaching for his war club he continued: *All
those hands you see hanging around this
wiigiwaam are the hands of your relatives who
came here to gamble. They thought as you are
thinking. They played and lost and their life was
the forfeit. I seek no one to come and gamble
with me but they that would gamble. Seek me
and whoever enters my lodge must gamble.
Remember, there is but one forfeit I demand of
those who gamble with me and lose, and that
forfeit is life. I keep the scalps and ears and*

*hands, the rest of the body I give to my friends
the wiindigoo and their spirits I consign to
niibaagiizis. I have spoken. Now we will play.*

At the conclusion of this speech, *naanabozho*
laughed long and heartily. This was unusual for
those who came there to gamble and the great
gambler felt very uneasy at the stolid
indifference of his guest.

Now, said the great gambler taking the
pagessewin — anishinaabe dish game — *here are
four figures — the four ages of man — which I
will shake in the dish four times. If they assume
a standing position each time, then I am the
winner. Should they fall, then I am the loser.*

Again *naanabozho* laughed a merry laugh
saying: *Very well, I will play, but it is customary
for the party who is challenged to play any game
to have the last play.* The great gambler
consented to do this. Taking up the dish he
struck it a sharp, quick blow on a spot prepared
for the purpose on the ground. The figures
immediately assumed a standing position. This
was repeated three times, and each time the
figures stood erect in the dish. But one chance
remained, upon which depended the destiny of
naanabozho and the salvation of the *anishinaabe*
people.

He was not frightened, and when the great evil
gambler prepared to make the final shake,
naanabozho drew near and when the dish came

down on the ground he made a whistle on the wind, as in surprise, and the figures fell. *Naanabozho* then seized the dish saying: *It is now my turn, should I win, you must die.*

Interpretive Notes

More than a century ago Henry Rowe
Schoolcraft, a student of geology and mineralogy,
named the *anishinaabeg* — the original people of
the woodland — the *ojibwa.* The meaning of the
word in the *anishinaabe* language is not certain,
but Schoolcraft reasoned that the root meaning
of the word *ojibwa* described the peculiar sound
of the *anishinaabe* voice.

George Copway — *kahgegagahbowh* — the
anishinaabe missionary explained that *the
people* were called the *ojibway* because of the
moccasins they wore which were "gathered on
the top from the tip of the toe, and at the
ankle."

In his book *The Traditional History and
Characteristic Sketches of the Ojibway Nation*,
published in London in 1850, *kahgegagahbowh*
wrote that "no other *indians* wore this style of
foot-gear, and it was on account of this
peculiarity that they were called *ojibway*, the
signification of which, is *gathering.*

William Warren takes exception with both
definitions of the word *ojibway.* In his *History of
the Ojibway Nation*, Warren, who was the first
person of *anishinaabe* ancestry to serve on the
Minnesota State Legislature, wrote the following

about the invented names:

"The word is composed of *ojib* — pucker up
— and *abwe* — to roast — and it means *to roast
till puckered up* . . .

"It is well authenticated by *their* traditions,
and by the writings of *their early white
discoverers*, that before *they* became acquainted
with, and made use of the fire arm and other
European weapons of war, instead of *their*
primitive bow and arrow and warclub, *their* wars
with other tribes were less deadly, and *they* were
more accustomed to secure captives, whom
under the uncontrolled feeling incited by
aggravated wrong, and revenge for similar
injuries, *they* tortured by fire in various ways.

"The name of *abwenag* — roasters — which
the *ojibways* have given to the *dakota* . . .
originated in their roasting their captives, and it
is as likely that the word *ojibwa* — to roast till
puckered up — originated in the same manner
. . .

"The name of the tribe has been most
commonly spelt, *chippeway*, and is thus laid
down in *our* different treaties with *them*, and
officially used by *our* Government."

But later Warren explained that the invented
names of the tribe do "not date far back. As a
race or distinct people they denominated
themselves *anishinaabe* . . . " He was obviously
identifying more with the thoughts of *his* white

discoverers than with the *anishinaabeg.*

Schoolcraft, who married an *anishinaabe* woman and became an official *indian* agent for the government, not only invented the name *ojibwa*, but he categorized the many families of the people of the woodland as the *algic* tribes. He invented the word *algic* from the word *algonguin*, which was a name invented earlier by the French to identify a different woodland tribe *they* had discovered. The word *algonquin* is still used to describe several tribes of the people who speak a similar language.

The story is told that the word *ojibwa* invented by Schoolcraft was misunderstood by a traveling bureaucrat who heard *chippewa* for *ojibwa.* Once recorded in treaties the name is a matter of law.

The *anishinaabeg* must still wear the invented names. The tragedy is that many young tribal people do not know the differences between the names. Some believe they are the *chippewa*, others know they are *anishinaabe.*

Almost a century ago, Frederick Baraga published the first dictionary of the *anishinaabe* language. Baraga, a latinist, interpreted *anishinaabemowin* according to old world linguistic structures.

The following *anishinaabe* words with definitions are quoted from the Baraga dictionary to show the confusion caused by the invented names for *the people:*

nind — the personal pronoun in *anishinaabemowin.*

nind ojibiwa — I write or mark on some object.

ojibiigan — writing, writ, document.

ojibiigewin — the act or art of writing.

odishkwagami — algonquin indian.

otchpiwe — chippewa indian.

nind otchipwem — I speak the chippewa language.

nind otchipwew — I am a chippewa indian.

otchipwemowin — the chippewa language.

anishinabe — human being, woman or child.

anishinabemowin — the indian language.

anishinabe ijitwawin — indian pagan religion.

anishinabe nagamon — indian song.

anishinabe ogima — indian agent.

nind anishinabewadis — I have the indian character, I am like an indian, I have feelings, principles, notions and dispositions like those of an indian.

nind anishinabe bimadis — I live like an indian.

nind anishinabem — I speak indian.

nind anishinabew — I am a human being, also, I am an indian.

Baraga defines *otchipwemowin* as the *chippewa* language and *anishinaabemowin* as the *indian* language and he defines *indian* as *anishinaabe*. There is of course no such language as the *indian* language because the word *indian* was also invented.

Today the people named the *odjibwa*, *otchipwe*, *ojibway*, *chippewa* and *chippeway*, still speak of themselves in the language of their hearts as the *anishinaabe*.

Not only have many tribal names been invented but the personal names of the people have been changed and translated without meaning. When a man is expected to know several thousand years of his history only in the language of the dominant society his identity is a dangerous burden.

Only two generations ago the *anishinaabeg* along with many other tribes, were systematically forbidden to speak their language and practice their religion. Now the people are summoned to be proud of their invented *indian* and *chippewa* heritage.

The cultural and political histories of the

anishinaabeg were written in the language of
those who invented the *indian*, renamed the
tribes, allotted the land, divided ancestry by
geometric degrees and categorized identity by
colonial reservations.

More than a century ago *kahgegagahbowh*, the
young *anishinaabe* christian missionary among
his own people, told the white readers of his
book that "communities can be governed by the
pure rules of christianity, with less coercion than
the laws of civilized nations, at present, imposed
upon their subjects . . .

"A vast amount of evidence can be adduced to
prove that force has tended to brutalize rather
than ennoble the *indian* race. The more man is
treated as a brother, the less demand for law . . .
*the less law there is, the more will man be
honored . . . "*

The song poems in this book are reexpressions
of the dreams of the *anishinaabeg* who believe
they will again be honored among men and share
the music of freedom.

Alan Merriam understood what *the people*
believe when he wrote " . . . every society has
occasions signaled by music which draw its
members together and reminds them of their unity."

In this book the *Anthropology of Music*,
Merriam wrote " . . . if music allows emotional
expression, gives aesthetic pleasure, entertains,
communicates, elicits physical response,

enforces conformity to social norms, and validates social institutions and religious rituals, it is clear that it contributes to the continuity and stability of culture."

About the turn of the century Frances Densmore traveled through the White Earth, Leech Lake and Red Lake *indian* reservations recording *anishinaabeg* songs on wax cylinders. The songs were later transcribed and published by the Smithsonian Institution, Bureau of American Ethnology, with literal translations and explanatory notes obtained from the individual *anishinaabe* singers.

Densmore wrote that the *anishinaabe* had no songs which were the "exclusive property of families or clans . . . a young man may learn his father's songs . . . but he does not inherit right to sing such songs, nor does his father force him to learn them . . .

"The melody is evidently considered more important than the words . . . the idea is the important thing, and this is firmly connected with the melody in the minds" of the *anishinaabeg.*

The *anishinaabe* singing voice has a characteristic wavering quality of tone. The singer sang alone or with the rhythm of the drum or rattle. The other musical instrument used by the *anishinaabeg* was the flute.

The illustrations in this book are enlarged

photographic reproductions of the original
anishinaabe pictomyths published about the turn
of the century by the Bureau of American
Ethnology in *Chippewa Music* by Frances
Densmore, *The Midewiwin or Grand Medicine
Society of the Ojibway* by W.J. Hoffman, and
Picture Writing of the American Indians by
Garrick Mallery.

The lyric poems and dream songs in this book
have been interpreted and reexpressed from the
original *anishinaabeg* song transcriptions
integrated with literal translations for the
Smithsonian Institution, Bureau of American
Ethnology, by Frances Densmore. Interpretive
notes about the song poems and pictomyths are
listed by page number.

The pictomyth on the title page resembles the
sun and represents the *midewiwin* secrets of the
heart.

The pictomyth opposite the table of contents
was reproduced from *The Midewiwin or Grand
Medicine Society of the Ojibway* by W.J.
Hoffman, published in 1891 by the Bureau of
American Ethnology. The tree is the center of
the earth after the first legendary destruction of
the earth when *naanabozho*, the cultural folk
hero of the *anishinaabeg*, escaped by climbing a
tree which grew ''above the surface of the
flood.'' Hoffman wrote that one member of the
midewiwin thought it ''related to a particular

medicinal tree which was held in estimation
beyond all others, and thus represented as the
chief of the earth.''

Page Notes

The *miigis* shell is the symbol of the spirit power of the *midewiwin.* The sacred shell resembles the cowrie and is frequently used to decorate *anishinaabe* ceremonial vestments. *Bawitig* is the *anishinaabe* descriptive name for the long rapids of St. Mary or Sault Ste. Marie, Michigan. Following the legendary *miigis* shell from the eastern sea the *anishinaabeg* gathered at *bawitig.* The sacred shell appeared for the last time at *mooningwanekaning* where *the people* established a community about five hundred years ago. In his history of the *ojibway,* Warren describes a copper plate with incised marks showing three *anishinaabeg* generations living at *mooningwanekaning* before contact was made with the new world discoverers. Warren wrote that he viewed the copper record of *the people* in the middle of the nineteenth century when it had eight incised marks. Warren estimated a generation at forty years.

Keeshkemun was an orator of the crane totem when the British military officers attempted to enlist the support of the *anishinaabeg* in the new world territorial wars.

The pictomyth in the introduction shows a candidate preparing for initiation into the *midewiwin.* The initiate is approaching the sacred medicine tree in the *midewiwin* lodge. Reproduced from *Chippewa Music* by Francis Densmore, published in 1910 by the Bureau of American Ethnology.

PAGE 21:
Densmore quoted an *anishinaabe* singer to explain this *midewiwin* pictomyth " . . . The circle is the earth. These three people live in the fourth layer under the earth; from there they sing.''

PAGE 23:
This pictomyth shows the sacred *midewiwin* stone and tree.

PAGE 25:
The *anishinaabeg* believe that the black crows arriving early in the spring brought the first rain to the prairie and woodland. The crow is also a symbol of wisdom.

PAGE 26:
This *midewiwin* pictomyth shows the spirit in the heart of the *anihsinaabe* singer. Hoffman wrote that the body of the singer was ''filled with knowledge relating to sacred medicines form the earth.''

PAGE 29:

In this song poem the singer feels the power of a summer storm in the woodland. Densmore wrote that the singer '' . . . hears the reverberation of the thunder and in his dream or trance he composes a song concerning it.''

The same person, identified by Densmore as *gagandac*, sang the following song. The musical notation is reproduced from *Chippewa Music* by Frances Densmore, published in 1910 by the Smithsonian Institution, Bureau of American Ethnology.

The title of the song poem is *The Approach of the*

Storm. The following is a translation by Densmore:

abitu	from the half
gicigun	of the sky
ebigwen	that which lives there
kabide bwewidun	is coming, and makes a noise

"The Thunder *manito* represents to the *indian* the mysterious spirit of the storm," Densmore wrote about the song, "and he imagines that this *manito* sometimes makes a voice to warn him of its approach. This is his interpretation of the distant thunder which precedes a storm. Hearing this, the *indian* hastens to put tobacco on the fire in order that the smoke may ascend as an offering or signal of peace to the *manito.* The idea which underlies the song is, *that which lives in the sky is coming and, being friendly, it makes a noise to let me know of its approach.*"

Densmore noted that "this means much less to the white race than to the *indian.* We are accustomed to noise; the *indian* habitually approaches in silence unless he wishes to announce his presence."

PAGE 30:
The thunderbird symbolizes thunder and

lightening in the mythology of many tribal
people. The pictomyth on this page shows the
spirit of the thunderbird flying in the sky.
Hoffman wrote that the thunderbird in this
pictomyth represents "a deity flying into the
arch of the sky. The short lines denote . . .
spirit lines . . . " or the place of the *manidoo*.
In another song poem the singer is surprised by
the thunderbirds or the large thunder clouds.
The *tchissakiwinini* receives his prophetic
powers from the thundergod or thunderbird.
Hoffman wrote that the *tchissakiwinini*
prognosticates the "success or misfortune of
hunters and warriors."

PAGE 31:
The melody in this song poem moves with
great freedom, Densmore wrote, forming "an
example of the strange personation which
characterizes many of the dream songs. In this
the singer contemplates the storm mystery of
the sky until he feels himself a part of it and
sings its song."

PAGE 35:
Many dream songs of the *anishinaabeg* are
dreams of flying as birds and clouds. The
singer of this song was watching a bird soaring
in the sky above him as he walked and
dreamed that he was walking in the sky with
the large bird.

PAGE 37:

The sky clears and the waters are smooth in
this song poem when the drum sounds for the
ceremonial initiation of a new member of the
midewiwin. Densmore wrote about this song
that "fair weather is symbolic of health and
happiness . . . the words of this song predict
health and happiness for the person to be
initiated." The expression *he hi hi hi* is the
sound of the feeling of the power of the sacred
spirit of the *midewiwin*. A *midewiwin* song is
completed with the syllables *ho ho ho ho*.

PAGE 39:

Densmore wrote that this dream song was
recorded by *maingans* — little wolf — who was
a member of the *midewiwin* and an
anishinaabe tchissakiwinini. Maingans
dreamed that he was summoned to the spirit
lodge of the big bear. Densmore quotes the
following narrative of the song by *maingans:*
"In my dream I went to the big bear's lodge
and he told me what to do. He told me how to
swallow bones and I often go back to his lodge
that I may learn from him again. This is what I
say in this song which I made up myself . . . "
The *tchissakiwinini* is an *anishinaabe* herbal
medicine and spirit healer. The spiritual power
of *tchissakiwinini* comes from the thunderbird

and dreams about animals. *Maingans* personal spiritual power comes from his dream songs about the big bear. The big bear is his spiritual teacher.

PAGE 40:
The *maang*, or loon totem, was an *anishinaabe* tribal family of leaders and orators. Densmore wrote that this song poem was sung before going into battle.

PAGE 41:
The spiritual power of the *midewiwin* gave the man shown in the pictomyth on this page the strength to live so old that he leans on a staff as he walks. The old man praises his age as spiritual power.

PAGE 43:
In this pictomyth the wavy lines from the mouth of the figure show the sound of speech or the spiritual power of a song.

PAGE 44:
The pictomyth on this page shows a dancing circle with *anishinaabeg* warriors at the bottom of the circle carrying *dakota* scalps on poles as they dance. In the center of the circle is the grave of an *anishinaabe* killed in battle.

Densmore wrote that the "poles bearing the scalps were stuck into the ground at the head of the grave, to stay there until the poles should decay and fall."

PAGE 45:
This song poem tells about an old *anishinaabe* woman who defended her family against an attack by the *dakota.* The story was told that the woman fought like a great bear, striking the woodland *dakota* warriors and tearing their canoe apart with her hands. The song poem on this page refers to the sound of *anishinaabeg* warriors dancing and playing as they return to their families. The men are happy and play a game as they return from battle.

PAGE 46:
Anishinaabeg children were taught to fear owls. Children were warned by their parents in songs and stories that the owls would catch them like mice if they left the dwelling place at night. The fear of owls kept the children home at night. There is a legend that *naanabozho* used the eyes of the owl to pass through the land of the sleeping sun on one of his many missions in the service of mankind. The onomatopoetic expression *gookookoo oo . . . gookookoo oo* — owl — is repeated in *anishinaabemowin.*

PAGE 48:
When an *anishinaabe* warrior was going into
battle he wore a small bird around his neck.
The bird skin was filled with a special herbal
medicine to protect him and give him courage.
This song poem is an avian dream of freedom
and safe flight into battle as the wind ruffles
the feathers of the bird.

PAGE 49:
Densmore wrote that this song poem was sung
at a dance in special honor of a warrior. It is
reexpressed here with special reference to
anishinaabeg people living today. The
pictomyth on this page shows an outline of the
manidoo — the *anishinaabe* spirit — which
appears as various animals in personal dream
songs.

PAGE 50:
Neniwa is the name of a man. This *midewiwin*
burial song was recorded by Densmore on the
White Earth *indian* reservation about the turn
of the century. The song was written by a man
to be sung after his death. Densmore wrote
that this pictomyth shows one of the
midewiwin spirits of the *anishinaabeg*.

PAGE 51:
The *anishinaabe* frequently hunted animals at

night with a light. George Copway —
kahgegagahbowh — wrote in his history of the
anishinaabeg how animals were held gazing at
the light of a birch bark lantern burning pitch,
while a hunter moved closer in his canoe for
the kill. The pictomyth with this song poem
shows a figure of a hunter gazing at the light of
a star.

PAGE 52:
In the woodland the shadberry was a common
refreshment among the *anishinaabeg.* The
shadberry or juneberry is a purplish fruit of the
shadbush. This song poem was recorded on the
White Earth *indian* reservation about the turn
of the century. Densmore wrote that the
anishinaabeg had a saying — take some
shadberries with you — when someone was
departing.

Not every *anishinaabe* family had a supply of
salt. Densmore wrote about this song poem
that in the Salt Treaty concluded at Leech
Lake in 1847 there was a stipulation that
members of the Pillager family of the
anishinaabe should receive five barrels of salt
annually for five years.

PAGE 53:
In this pictomyth the varying lines from the

mouth of the figure show the sound of a song poem. It is believed that this love song was composed at *mooningwanekaning* — Madeline Island. The *anishinaabe* interjection *nia* is used instead of *ah*, *oh*, or *alas*, which have been used in previous translations. In *anishinaabemowin*, *nia* is a feminine exclamation.

PAGE 55:
The singer hopes to find a lover who will see her as beautiful as the roses. The rose is her *solucination*. The pictomyth with the song poem shows a heart in a figure surrounded with roses. Densmore wrote: the ''love charms is a very popular form of magic'' among the *anishinaabeg*.

   The singer of this love charm told the story of the song to Densmore at the Red Lake *indian* reservation about the turn of the last century. ''She consented with reluctance,'' Densmore wrote for the Bureau of American Ethnology, ''as it was the summer season and she said that snakes would certainly bite her at night if she told stories in the summer . . . '' Densmore described the woman in her sixties as the ''most dirty and unattractive woman with whom the writer has come in contact . . . with coy shyness she said the song meant that she was as beautiful as the roses. She also drew a crude picture of the song.''

The varying lines coming from the body of the figure in the song pictomyth below show the feeling of a man for the singer of the following song poem recorded and translated by Densmore:

i can charm the man
he is completely
fascinated by me

In the pictomyths of the *midewiwin*, lines are drawn from the body and heart of a figure to show spiritual strength and intuitive feeling.

PAGE 58:
In this song poem the lover of the singer has returned to *bawitig.* Densmore wrote that the singer was the sister of William Warren the *anishinaabe* historian. The Warrens were of *anishinaabe* and French ancestry and lived at *mooningwanekaning* in the early nineteenth century. The family was active in the fur trade and later moved to the White Earth *indian* reservation.

PAGE 59:
In this pictomyth the five varying lines show different sounds of the voice of the singer. A gift usually accompanied an invitation to dance among the *anishinaabeg.* Densmore wrote that it was the custom for *anishinaabeg* women to give the first invitation to dance. In this song poem the singer has been waiting for her lover to return her invitation as they sit around the drum across from each other.

PAGE 60:
A brass kettle obtained in trade for fur was of great value to the *anishinaabeg.* In this song poem a woman representing her son is offering her big brass kettle.

PAGE 61:
Densmore wrote that the two figures in this

pictomyth show the *manidoo* religious spirit of the *anishinaabeg*. The horizontal figure is the *waaban manidoo*, the east spirit, and the upright figure is the *zhaawans manidoo*, the south spirit. *Naanabozho* is the *anishinaabe* trickster and cultural folk hero who disguises himself in many living things to explain and justify through imagination the conflicts of experience in tribal life. Songs and stories about *naanabozho* explain the meaning of living things and human behavior. *Nanabozho* stories answer the questions a child is likely to ask about his world. In this song poem *naanabozho* invited the ducks to sing and dance on the water. He told them they must keep their eyes closed. While the ducks were dancing with their eyes closed *naanabozho* went about tying string to their legs. The story tells about an easy way to hunt ducks and the song poem explains why diving ducks have red eyes — some peeked — and why ducks fly in formations - because *naanabozho* tied them together.

Stith Thompson in his work on mythology explained that one duck discovered the old *naanabozho* dance trick and got away tailless and red eyed. Diving ducks not only have red eyes but short tails because *naanabozho* caught them by the tail feathers.

The *anishinaabeg* seldom told stories about *naanabozho* in the summer for fear that the trickster would be present and listening in some living form. It was safe to tell *naanabozho* tales in the winter when he is not likely to be around as a plant or small animal.

The pictomyth on the cover shows the man who speaks and the man who listens. The picture was originally incised on a *midewiwin* birch bark scroll and reproduced in a book published by the Bureau of American Ethnology.

PAGE 63:
The varying line from the figure in the pictomyth on this page shows the voice of the *midewiwin* singer reaching to the sky and making the day bright and clear.

PAGE 71:
In this pictomyth rain is falling from the sky. Densmore wrote that the two ovals in the picture represent water or two lakes. The figure in the picture holds a sacred *midewiwin* drum in one hand and in the other hand a stick for beating the drum.

PAGE 99:
Densmore wrote that this pictomyth suggests
the birchbark container used by the
anishinaabeg for storing wild rice during the
winter.

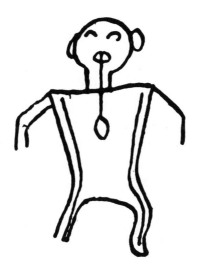

Anishinaabemowin Glossary

The orthographic transcriptions of *anishinaabemowin* words in this glossary are the same as those in *Ojibwewi-Ikidowinan: An Ojibwe Word Resource Book*, by John Nichols and Earl Nyholm. The definitions of the selected words listed here are based on those in *Ojibwe-Ikidowinan* and those translated more than a century ago in *A Dictionary of the Otchipew Language*, by Frederick Baraga.

aadizookaan, plural *aadizookaanag.* Traditional story.

akiwenzii. Old man.

amik; plural, *amikwag.* Beaver.

animosh; plural, *animoshag.* Dog.

anishinaabe; plural, *anishinaabeg.* Ojibwe, or
    Chippewa, person.

anishinaabekwe, anishinaabe. Woman.

anishinaabemowin. Oral language of the *anishinaabe.*

apaakozigan. Inner bark of red osier dogwood, mixed
with tobacco.

apakweshkway. Cattail mat.

asekaan. Tanned hide.

asemaa. Tobacco.

ataage. He who bets or gambles.

bakaan. Different.

bakaan ishkode. Different fire. Baraga noted that for a
woman *nin bakan-ishkotawe* means "I am in
my monthly flowings," or more accurately, "I
make my fire elsewhere, not in the lodge" (as
the women used to do at the time of their
monthly flowings).

bangishimog. To the west, in the west.

bapakine. Grasshopper.

bawitig. Rapids in a river (according to Baraga).

bibigwan. Flute.

biboon. It is winter.

bishigwaadaajimo. He tells a sexy story.

chimookomaan. chi, big or great, and *mookomaan,*
knife; or white man. The name is derived from
a description of the first white men, who wore
swords or carried long knives: the men with the
big knives. *chimookomaan* is the same as
gichimookomaan, meaning white men or large

knives. Nichols and Nyholm listed *waabishkizi* as "he is white," *waabishkaa* as "it is white," and the word *waabaabigan* as "white clay, or white earth." Baraga noted that *waiabishkiwed* is the *anishinaabe* word for white person.

dibaajimowin. Story, narration of events.

geget. Surely, indeed, certainly.

gichi. Big or great.

gichimakwa. Great bear.

gichimanidoo. Great spirit.

gichimookomaan. White man, large knife.

gichi nitaa ataage, gichi nita ataaged. Gichi, great; *Nitaa,* knows how to, or is skillful at; *ataaged,* the great gambler; *ataage,* he who bets or gambles, or the great gambler, in *anishinaabe* stories.

gichiziibi. The big river, Mississippi River.

giiwebiboon. It is late winter.

giiwedin. North, to the north.

giiweniibin. It is late summer.

giizis. Son, moon, month.

gimiwan. It is raining.

gookooko oo. Owl.

ikwe. Woman, female.

ikwe manidoo. Spirit woman.

inaabandam. He dreams, he has a vision.

inini. Man, male.

ishkode. Fire.

jiigibiig. Along the shore, by the water. Baraga
translated *tchigibig* as "on the beach, on the
lake shore, near the lake on the shore."

maang. Loon.

maji. Bad. Baraga noted that *matchi* means "bad, evil,
ill, wicked, malignant, malicious, mean, vicious,
unfit." He lists *matchimashkiki*, for example, as
"evil medicine, that is, poison, venom."

majimanidoo. Bad spirit, devil. Baraga noted that
matchi manito means an "evil spirit, devil,
satan." Nichols and Nyholm entered five
anishinaabe words under *maji.* Bishop Baraga
listed twenty-seven words under *matchi,*
apparently expressing a religious preoccupation
with the notion of evil spirits and tribal demons.

makade. Black, or black gunpowder.

makade mashkikiwaaboo. Coffee.

makadewikonayewinini. Priest. Baraga listed
makatewikwanaie as "the priest, he that wears
black clothes." *Makatewiiass* was translated as
"Negro, mulatto, colored man." Nichols and
Nyholm listed *makadewiiyaas* as "Negro,"
makadewizi as "he is black," and
makadewaanzo as "he is colored black."

Makade is translated as "black," and *wiiyaas* as "meat."

makade ziibe. Black river

makizin. Moccasin, shoe.

makizinataage. Moccasin game; he plays the moccasin game.

makwa. Bear.

manidoo. God, spirit.

manidoo giizis. The month of January.

manoomin. Wild rice.

mashkiki. Medicine.

mashkikiiwikwe. Nurse.

mashkikiiwinini. Doctor.

mazinaigan. Book, paper, document.

mazhiwe. He has sexual intercourse.

memengwaa. Butterfly.

midewigaan. The lodge of the *midewiwin.*

midewiwin. The medicine dance and healers of the *anishinaabe.*

miigis. The sacred cowrie of the *anishinaabe.*

miigwani wiiwakwaan. Feather headdress.

mindimooye. Old lady, old woman.

mishiike. Turtle. Baraga noted that *mishike* means a "kind of large tortoise." The editor of *The Progress* translated *mechekans* as "king of the turtles."

missameg. The whale (Baraga).

mitig. Tree, stick.

mitigwakik. The sacred drum of the *midewiwin.*

mookomaan. Knife.

mooningwane. Yellow-shafted flicker.

naanabozho. The trickster in *anishinaabe* stories.

nagamon. Song.

nibi. Water.

niibin. It is summer.

niiyawee. Namesake (Baraga).

niijii. My friend, my brother; *niijikiwe,* my female
        friend.

niikaanis. My friend, my brother.

noodin. Wind; it is windy.

noodin manidoo. Spirit of the wind.

nookomis. Grandmother.

oodena. Town.

tchigibig. "On the beach, on the lake shore," as
        translated by Baraga.

tchissakan. Juggler's lodge. Baraga translated
        tchissakin as, "I perform the Indian jugglery, in
        order to know the future, or to know events that
        happened at a distance."

tchissakiwin. Indian jugglery; to know the future or
        distant events. Baraga translated
        tchissakiwinini as "juggler."

waaban. It is dawn; east, in the east.

waabaabigan. White clay, white earth.

waawaatesi. Firefly.

wadiswan. The nest of a bird.

wemitigoji, wemitigoozhi. Frenchman.

wiigiwaam. Wigwam, lodge.

wiigwass. Birchbark.

wiigwassi jiimaan. Birchbark canoe.

wiigwaasi mitig. White birchbark.

wiindigoo. The evil cannibal in *anishinaabe* stories.

wiinitoo. Dirties it up. Karl May, the nineteenth
century German novelist, named his exotic,
heroic tribal warrior Winnetou, although he was
an ersatz chief of the Apaches.

wiisaakodewikwe. Mixedblood female.

wiisaakodewinini. Mixedblood male.

zhaaganaash, jaganash. Englishman, according to
Baraga.

zhaawan, jawan. South.

ziibi. River.

ziigwan. It is spring.

ziizibaakwad. Sugar; originally, maple sugar.

ziizibaakwadaaboo. Maple sap.

zoogipo. It snows.